MW01493800

Astral Projection for Beginners

The Astral Travel Guide to an Intentional Out-of-Body Experience

Free Bonus from Silvia Hill available for limited time

Hi Spirituality Lovers!

My name is Silvia Hill, and first off, I want to THANK YOU for reading my book.

Now you have a chance to join my exclusive spirituality email list so you can get the ebooks below for free as well as the potential to get more spirituality ebooks for free! Simply click the link below to join.

P.S. Remember that it's 100% free to join the list.

~~$27~~ FREE BONUSES

- 9 Types of Spirit Guides and How to Connect to Them
- How to Develop Your Intuition: 7 Secrets for Psychic Development and Tarot Reading
- Tarot Reading Secrets for Love, Career, and General Messages

Access your free bonuses here
https://livetolearn.lpages.co/sh-astral-projection-for-beginners-paperback/

Contents

Introduction

So, you want to learn how to leave your body. The first time you heard about this, it was probably from that one kooky uncle of yours. He watches Gaia and insists there are reptilians and grays among us, so you had a hard time taking him seriously. Until, for whatever reason, you decided to look into this stuff, and you began to wonder how a whole lot of people could buy into the craziness. Maybe you started to notice a common thread with all the stories and decided there may be something to it after all.

Or, you may already have experience with the supernatural and paranormal and want another way to interact with the worlds beyond what we can sense. Perhaps you just saw this book, and for no particular reason, you decided it was next on your reading list. Either way, you made the right call picking this book.

There are far too many lies and myths surrounding the phenomenon of astral projection. It's tough to tell the difference between fact and fiction, especially if you've never even had a lucid dream before, let alone left your physical body. So, I've written this book to help you explore the wonderful world of the astral realm with confidence and a spirit of adventure.

Hop onto Google or another search engine, and type "astral projection." Once upon a time, you'd see a few results that could help you achieve it. Now, page one of those search results is packed full of Amazon ads. Right beneath those ads are a bunch of articles and blogs trying their hardest to convince you it's all in your head. "It's just a load of crap," they say. Or you find reviews of a show on Netflix with a premise that does more harm than good to the aspiring astral traveler. So, this book just had to be written because I felt a personal responsibility to fix that mess.

Other books tell you about the astral realm, give you one or two ways to check it out, and then leave you to your own devices. This one will take you by the hand and walk you through everything you need to know, from exit to re-entry.

Many of the best books on astral projection are sadly outdated and unnecessarily complicated, putting readers off the subject altogether. You'll find this book is a beginner-friendly and straightforward read, which will help you understand what the astral plane is and how to get there. You'll learn how to prepare your mind and body for your journeys, and the best methods to use that will give you successful projections every time.

We'll go over how to make your way through the astral plane without feeling like a total klutz and how to work through the various issues that can pop up along your journey. You'll also learn the correct way to return to your body. And we'll throw in a fantastic bonus, too. A 30-day calendar of affirmations, meditations, and mindfulness exercises that will put you on the path to successful astral projections on demand.

Part One: Astral Projection Basics

Chapter One: Understanding the Astral

If you're going to take a trip to a foreign country you've never been to before, then it makes sense for you to learn all you can about it. The same thing applies to the astral plane. The last thing you want is to take a trip somewhere, only to find your clothes are all wrong. Or that you're doing everything the natives find disrespectful (without meaning to, of course).

"The World in a Grain of Sand"

There is a lovely poem, "Auguries of Innocence," by William Blake, which begins with these lines:

> *To see a World in a grain of sand*
>
> *And a Heaven in a Wild Flower*
>
> *Hold Infinity in the palm of your hand*
>
> *And Eternity in an hour*

Those lines are the most beautiful and apt description of the astral plane. First things first, though. The world you know is not the only one. Now, it's easy to assume that this statement isn't true. After all, we live in times where science is king—and while that's not a bad thing, it does mean that unless you can observe a phenomenon physically, it doesn't exist. You could say that scientists are the true pioneers of the phrase, "Pics, or it didn't happen." Sure, there are those scientists who dared to explore topics considered "fringe." However, we're still a long way from the level of open-mindedness we need to make more progress in exploring consciousness.

The physical world you're in right now is but a teeny, tiny part of all of existence. Some things exist outside of waking awareness, which you cannot perceive unless you tune to the right frequency of consciousness. The trouble is, we've all been taught that there is nothing to life but the material things you can detect with your five senses.

Right from when you were a kid, your parents told you that your dreams were not real, and that your friend who cheered you up when you were down was only imaginary. Most of us heard this enough that we bought into the lie. However, some of us were fortunate enough to have had experiences that caused us to wonder, even into adulthood, "What if there's more?" Chances are you've had an experience that has led you to this book. So, you should know right now: you're not crazy. There is more to life than meets the eye.

Let's get back to William Blake's poem, so you can grasp the idea of what the astral plane is. Imagine you're holding a grain of sand and in that single grain is the Earth, all other known planets, and our universe. Now, imagine standing on the beach. Try to grasp the fact that all that sand is a universe of universes.

Think about the idea of having all of infinity, or timelessness, in the palm of your hand. In the astral plane, you could experience an entire lifetime, only to return to the physical and find that just ten minutes have gone by. I should mention that this is not always the case, though, as you can wind up in a section of the plane that closely matches physical reality and time.

The Astral Plane

You can pick up your car keys and drive to the mall, but you can't just visit the astral plane without the proper vehicle because it's outside of our 3D world.

Some believe that when you die, you leave your physical body and go to the astral plane. People think it's a spiritual waiting room, of sorts, between heaven and Earth. From this point, you can either return to Earth for another game of "Being Human," or you can ascend to higher planes of existence.

The truth is, you function on more planes of existence than just the material and the astral. Still, your waking consciousness is primarily focused here on Earth. The astral is beyond the physical; it is the world of psychic phenomena, spirits, and dreams. It connects your material world to your rich, mystical one.

Sufism, Kabbalah, and Spiritualism all acknowledge the existence of the astral realm. Likewise, the New Age Movement, Theosophy, and Eckankar have philosophies centered on it.

Helena Petrovna Blavatsky, one of the founders of the Theosophical Society, put forward the idea of Masters, also called Mahatmas. They are human, or used to be human, and have now transcended from the Earth realm to the astral.

Paul Twitchell's Eckankar is also called the Ancient Science of Soul Travel. Just as the name implies, initiates are taught various ways to commune with the astral realm and communicate with the Masters. The latter exist there to offer guidance, healing, strength, wisdom, and whatever else one may need to make it through the grueling grind of life on Earth. The students of Eckankar, called chelas, learn how to experience the Sugmad (God) by traveling along the Audible Life Current called the Eck, which flows to and from the Sugmad. The goal for the chela isn't astral travel but to finally make their way to the Sugmad.

The New Age Movement is a beast with many heads. While there are various beliefs and methodologies for getting in touch with the worlds beyond this one, they all share a common belief in the astral plane. Some schools of thought believe you can only go to the astral realm when you die, or in a dream. However, most New Agers experience this plane while alive by deliberately inducing lucid dreams or astral projections—which are also called out-of-body experiences (OBEs), soul travel, or astral travel. Other ways to get to the astral plane include meditation and near-death experiences (NDEs). The latter is something you should definitely *not* try to induce, please.

The astral dimension comprises seven key levels or planes. Each plane has its own variety of sub-planes and on and on. It may sound like you could get lost in there, but that's nothing to worry about, since one way or another, you will return to your body after every exploration. This plane of existence covers the entire material world, and yet, it does not exist spatially. Instead, it vibrates at a much higher frequency than our material world.

Think of the astral plane as the world's tallest skyscraper—but infinitely taller. Every floor is a sub-plane in the astral, with its own unique qualities, occupants, rules, physics, and energy. The floors closer to the bottom are of lower vibrations. Now, "lower" isn't necessarily bad; it just means that the energy here is denser. These planes are closest to the Earth. Chances are, when you first leave your body, this is where you will wind up. You'll find other projectors like you, as well as those who actually live in these planes.

All Your Bodies

You have at least six arms, six legs, and three heads. Before you go feeling around for them, allow me to clarify. You have three bodies:

- Physical
- Astral

● Causal

Your physical body is also called your gross body. No, not "gross" as in ugly, but as in obvious. You can see it. You already know what your physical body looks like, so I'll spare you a recap of Biology 101. It's the body you use to do everyday human things in this ordinary human world.

According to Vedanta, this body is called the **Sthula Sarira** and has three major phases: *Sambhava*, which is birth; **Jara,** meaning old age; and *Maranam*, or death. In addition, this body has five elements; *Vayu* or air, *Prithvi* or Earth, *Agni* or fire, *Apas* or water, and *Akasha* or ether. To replenish these elements, we must eat right, practice mindfulness and meditation, and consider yoga. The practice has poses that recharge each element of your body. Upon death, the elements split from one another.

Your astral body is the body that has your energy centers or chakras. In Vedanta, it is the **Suksma Sarira**. This is your energy body, the one that connects you with All That Is, or the stuff of life itself. This life is also called Prana or Qi. It keeps your physical body functioning correctly. When your mind is clouded with negative thoughts and emotions, the life force can't move freely through your body.

This body has emotional thought and vital power. When you're awake, you may have a hard time connecting to the astral body. However, when you're fast asleep and dreaming, you move about primarily in your astral body. With this body, you can feel pain or pleasure. It's intricately connected to your senses, intellect, and mind. It helps you with involuntary body functions like metabolism, breathing, digestion, and circulation. It keeps your brain, skeletal, and muscular health in check as well.

This body is usually modeled off your physical one, but there's no need for it to maintain that shape and form. I remember the first OBE I had when I realized I could see all around me at once. It was not because I had eyes all over my head, but because what we really are is consciousness. While on previous travels, I saw things as though I was looking through my regular eyes. On this occasion, I was able to see the entire room from multiple angles at the same time. That's just one of the mind-blowing phenomena you can experience during your astral explorations.

Another intriguing thing about being in your astral body is that you will realize the power of your thoughts. You will witness them come to life and notice things adapting as quickly as you change your mind about them. When you begin your practice, observe this thought power you possess and realize that this is exactly how the physical world works. The only difference is that your thoughts must move through space and time to manifest on Earth.

Your causal body possesses all the information about you and your many lives, present and past. It is the **Karana Sarira.** You can connect with your causal body from a place of deep sleep where thoughts or emotions do not bog you down. This body has all the data on your desires, hopes, fears, and perceptions. It's called the "causal" body because it affects your waking consciousness, as well as your dream states. Upon death, the causal and astral bodies leave the physical ones.

Resembling light, the astral body is already tricky enough to perceive from waking consciousness. The causal one is even more subtle than the astral one. It holds a record of all karmas from all your lives. It is thanks to the information it has that you have the character you do right now. The Creator works through the causal body to connect with us all, giving us divine revelations on how to live a joyful life—if we could only listen!

This doctrine of three bodies is held in high regard in Hindu philosophy. The physical body, which survives on food, is the frailest and the first to go. The astral body thrives on emotions, thoughts, and feelings. Therefore, it can go on for much longer. Finally, the causal body lives the longest, receiving life from the process of discovering one's self, as well as peace. Just so you know, there's no more terrific way to find yourself than to interact with the astral realm.

Mind: Cementing Your Bodies

Before you reach out for a glass of juice, you first think about doing it in your mind. You see yourself reaching out, feel the cool glass, hold it, and put it to your lips in your mind before you make an actual move physically. The same applies when it comes to your mental and causal bodies. You can't work any of your bodies without using your mind.

Sadly, a lot of people assume they cannot control their thoughts and emotions. They believe every thought they have is true. Without question, they accept those thoughts and the feelings that arise with them, even when doing that doesn't serve them. You must understand that the mind is a tool. It is a machine meant to serve you. If you're going to enjoy your astral journeys, and grow on account of them, then you need to know that your mind is a tool you use.

You are not your hands, feet, or eyes, yet you use these things like tools. You must see your mind the same way and master it. Remember I mentioned that the astral plane is very sensitive to thought? You can surely see why it pays to be in control of your mind. To be a successful astral traveler, you should train your mind to accept that soul travel is a safe and easy thing for you to do. This way, you have a greater chance of success. Your mind can achieve amazing feats because Source is quite literally the source of its power.

Most people allow their minds to run wild, sometimes to the point where they wish they could escape their own heads. If you can relate to this feeling, know that you can take back control. The first step is to realize that *you are not your mind.* The next thing you need to do is understand *the thoughts in your mind are only true IF you accept them as true.*

Who Are You?

So, you've just found out that you have at least three bodies—five if we go with Sadhguru's explanation: the physical, mental, energy, etheric (astral), and bliss bodies. On top of that, you've just learned that you're not your mind. You're not your body either. That will understandably leave you wondering about your true identity. For you to traverse the subtler worlds, you must know who you are. You are the Source itself, having a never-ending adventure here on Earth as a human being.

Like Maharaj Jagat Singh explains in *The Science of the Soul*, your soul came down into the realm of the mind and then moved further away from its real self until it forgot who it really was. It forgot that it is Alpha and Omega, undying. It chose instead to think of itself as a body. It went from being the causal body in the causal plane to identifying as the astral body in a realm full of illusion. Finally, it came down to the material world, clothed in flesh, in addition to its astral and causal coverings. For this reason, the soul's light is usually dim in this world. Many would call you a nut-job if you suggested that they are not their bodies, minds, identities, job titles, names, and so on.

Dim as the light of most souls are, the fact is you can't snuff out that light completely. Night after night, we still dream. We transcend our physical bodies to carry on other activities in nonphysical realms. It's just that some people are aware of their travels and what they do during these times, while others are not. You're reading this book, which means you would like to master your astral life. Deciding to become aware of the other aspects of yourself is a solid choice. With dedication and patience, you will enjoy all the benefits of your increased awareness in everyday life.

Chapter Two: What Is Astral Projection?

Now let's talk about astral projection—not the Israeli band that plays psychedelic trance, but the phenomenon itself. Astral projection, or astral travel, is the process of deliberately having an out-of-body experience. It is the separation of the astral body from the physical one to travel on the astral plane.

While the term was coined by the Theosophists of the 19th century, this phenomenon is as old as humans and spans various cultures. In addition, there are multiple means to achieve astral travel. For example, some use meditation, and others use relaxation and visualization techniques and hypnosis. Finally, some use hallucinogens, but that is outside the scope of this book and not recommended.

Sadhguru talks about astral projection as removing your etheric body from the physical one. Since it's such a hot topic these days, some charlatans push the idea that it's just about lying down and visualizing or imagining you're out of your body. That's not it at all. Astral projection isn't imagination. You will feel a definite sense of yourself stepping out of your physical body. You will be able to see your body on the bed or chair or wherever you left it—in the most literal sense of the word "see." There is no make-believe here.

Remember, you're none of your bodies, and you're not your mind either. As weird as that sounds, it's true. What you are, at your very core, is pure consciousness. So you see, when you astral project, you turn your awareness from the physical plane to focus on the astral one through the astral body.

When you use the proper techniques, you will be able to leave your body and go wherever you please. You can visit physical locations worldwide or locations that aren't known to us here on Earth. You can fly through the clouds, or my personal favorite, take a trip to outer space, where the colors of every star and planet burst with color and life. You can connect with other astral travelers or heal yourself or a loved one. You can receive inspiration for your next book or painting or receive instruction from your guides on issues that matter to you. You can gain clarity about what you should be doing with your life or even take a peek at what the future may have in store for you or the world as a whole.

You can do all of this and more because the astral realm is the 5th dimension of life, meaning this realm is outside the confines of time and space. Therefore, past, present, and future exist in the interminable now, so you can learn what you want.

Astral Projection versus Lucid Dreaming

Lucid dreaming and astral projection are both fantastic, yet they are not the same. Lucid dreams are subjective. They are your own experiences and allow you to play with infinite scenarios. However, astral projection is objective because the planes you visit really do exist, and much like in the physical realm, they have their own limits and laws.

Lucid dreaming happens when you wake up in your dreams. Dreams can be pretty absurd and nonsensical. You could be running around the street in your birthday suit demanding to see the Prince of Timbuktu, and you wouldn't think it strange. The reason is that when you sleep, your brain's critical faculties also take a break. This means you don't question any of the weirdness going on. Lucidity is achieved when you wake up in your dream and realize, "Hey, I'm dreaming!"

Typically, when people realize they're lucid in a dream and haven't had much practice controlling their minds, they get a little too excited. Unfortunately, this excitement causes them to slip back into thinking the dream is real or waking up completely.

Here's something super cool you should know. You can astral project *from* a lucid dream. All you have to do is intend to find your physical body, and you're now astral projecting. Whatever you do, don't get too close to your body, or you'll probably wake up. Also, you may experience a strange sense of bilocation, meaning you can feel you are two people, in two bodies (astral and physical) at once. With practice, you should find it easy to shift your awareness to the astral one, so you can get on with your travels.

Astral projection is a whole other thing. You don't dream. You enter into a state where your mind is awake and your body asleep, and then you perform the exit procedure that works best. You will experience your astral body separating itself from your sleeping form. Again, nothing about this is imagination. You will feel actual vibratory sensations, hear loud sounds, maybe voices, maybe singing. When you're astral projecting, you will know it without a doubt.

In a lucid dream, you can control everyone and everything around you. For example, you could turn the sky yellow or build an entire airplane out of marshmallows. You can make someone look like a clown or an ant. There's nothing off limits to you.

When it comes to astral projection, the only things you can manipulate like this are all things that have to do with yourself. You can change how you look, give yourself a different body or face, conjure up tools you need, and so on. However, you can't control the people and other entities you run into because they have free will like you. Like you, they are sentient beings. Just like you wouldn't appreciate someone trying to dictate your life, they don't like that either. When it comes to the environment, you may find it's not easy for you to control it by issuing commands. You'd need to generate energy by using your intention to get them to do your bidding.

Spontaneous Projections versus Deliberate Projections

Deliberate astral projection, obviously, happens when the traveler consciously decides to go visiting that plane. There's planning involved, and you know exactly what you're going to do when you come out of your body.

Now let's address spontaneous travels. I was drawn to the exploration of consciousness because I had my very first projection as a kid. It was unexpected, and it was pretty scary, but only because I was unaware of what was going on at the time. Before that experience, I would often have trouble with sleep paralysis, which is when your mind wakes up before your body does, and you can't move. The reason that happens is that when you sleep, your body shuts down all nonessential motor functions so that you don't act out your dreams. So, when your mind is up and your body hasn't noticed, you just stay there, unable to move. Had I known then what I do now, I would have begun my exploration a lot sooner!

My experience was frightening because I could see my body, and I was floating up and away from it toward the ceiling. By the time I got to the ceiling, the fear magnified by a hundred as I thought to myself, "So this is how I die. I'm not ready for judgment."

Coming from a religious background that involved a lot of guilt-tripping, you can see how scary the idea of death must have been to a teenager. With that thought, I felt a force like a giant hand shove my astral body back down, and I rejoined my physical body.

I knew it was real because everything in the room looked and sounded the same, and I was lying in the same weird position I was in—coffin style. It took about ten years for me to get the courage to research what had happened to me. It turns out, it was a spontaneous astral projection. You don't plan for them to happen. They just do, whether you want them to or not.

Have you ever felt strange, intense vibrations coursing through your body when you wake up a little, in the middle of the night, too tired to get out of bed? Or have you ever experienced the phenomenon of sleep paralysis? Then know that each of those times, you came really close to having a spontaneous astral projection.

Sometimes, during these spontaneous projections (as well as deliberate ones), you may receive help from another being or traveler with leaving your body. They may grab your hands or your feet to help you out. (Other times, no one's helping, and it's just hypnagogic hallucinations). However, because most people are unfamiliar with the astral and how the mind works with it, they become terrified. That fear causes them to misinterpret what's happening. What may have been a benevolent being helping you is misconstrued as a demon trying to yank you down to hell or something.

Scientific Proof of Astral Projection

December 1, 2011, the CIA partly declassified a sanitized copy of a document on astral projection. During the Cold War, the traveler was tasked to journey to the USSR to locate a specific facility. They found it and gave the precise coordinates of its location. The traveler also provided many valuable details about what it looked like on the outside. For example, they said there were dish antennas, helicopter pads, and other things on site. The traveler also learned that in addition to receiving the Soviet satellite's downlink, the antennas were also used to intercept downlink from US satellites.

Now for the moment of truth. The CIA went to find this facility, and they did. Even though there were different numbers of dish antennas in various dimensions from what the traveler shared, they were there all the same.

In another double-blind experiment, the CIA gave the traveler coordinates of a little island in the Indian Ocean occupied by the Soviets. The experimenters did not have this location on their map. They even thought that the traveler would encounter nothing but water—until the subject began to draw a map on a large scale, needing more and more sheets of paper. When they were done, the CIA put all the sheets together, and what they found was a precise match of the island. It was such an accurate drawing that it also detailed the topography of the island. The traveler was also able to tell the CIA exactly what was going on over there. These are just two of the experiments with astral travel documented by the CIA.

Do a quick Google search about astral projection. You'll find so many trying to discredit it, from those who say, "Well, it both is and isn't real," to those who flat out stamp it as a pseudoscience not worthy of exploring. Actual astral travelers find the confidence with which naysayers dismiss this phenomenon to be mind-boggling at worst and hilarious at best. However, the skepticism is understandable, since this is one thing that a person needs to experience themselves to accept it as valid. Without personal experience, skeptics think of astral travelers as insane. If they're polite, they'll say something like it's just the neurons in your brain doing "neuron-y stuff."

Suppose you're willing to go past page one of Google (or use a different search engine altogether) to dig into research that doesn't start out trying to disparage or disprove astral travel. In that case, you will find a lot of information that proves OBEs can be verified scientifically. Skeptics should consider that the scientific community deemed lucid dreams "unreal" until as recently as four decades ago.

To look deeper into this phenomenon, you should check out books by Robert Monroe, Robert Bruce, Hereward Carrington, Oliver Fox, Sylvan Muldoon, and Graham Nicholls. These pioneers are why modern-day astral travelers have made such great strides in their discoveries about the astral realm and the mechanics of leaving the body. Moreover, they were unafraid to explore this "fringe" matter during times when conventional science and religion were even less accepting of taboo subjects like this than they are now. Hence, we owe them a world of gratitude.

Mind Is Key

I have already touched on this subject before, but it's so vital that it bears repeating. Your mental habits and ability to control your mind will significantly serve you when you begin astral travel. Here's why you need to keep your mind "in mind," so to speak, before you start your journey.

1. **You must mentally accept that you _can_ leave your body.** If you don't buy into this, you're simply making the process a whole lot more complicated. Ask yourself why you're fighting the idea. It could be a result of fears that you have about the phenomenon. Those fears will be addressed soon enough. Once you understand what you're getting into you will know there's no reason to be afraid. Your mind will be more receptive. You need to realize that many of the horror stories you read about astral travel resulted from the state of mind that the projectors were in. Fearful minds attract experiences to be afraid of. Remember that.

2. **You must be in the right frame of mind when you project.** For example, suppose you've had a terrible day at work. In that case, you're stressed out, anxious about something, feeling angry or hateful. You shouldn't be traveling to the astral plane in that state of mind. There's a big chance that everything you encounter in the astral world will be of a low energy vibration, which means more

frightening experiences for you to contend with. When this happens, the odds are you'll never want to project again, and your mind will run with that and always shut it down no matter what.

3. Your mind is the chief way you can control things in the astral world. Forget about physics. Your mind is the way you move and determines your experiences. Think about flying, and you're doing it. Want to go somewhere? Think of being there, and there you are. Think of seeing someone, and there they are. So, it only makes sense that when you encounter scary-looking beings, letting your mind feast on fear will make everything worse.

In summary, your mind's job is to help you realize you can project. It's also supposed to help you relax enough to allow the phenomenon to happen and keep you in control of your reactions and impulses in the astral.

Another thing is that most first-time travelers get so excited at seeing their bodies that they're drawn right back in before they can explore. It's understandable to be excited, but you want to keep that in check and remain calm. The way to do that is to rehearse the whole trip in your mind. See it through from start to finish, refining whatever details you must. The more you imagine seeing your sleeping form, the less novel it will be when you finally do leave your body. If you don't get sucked right back in, that gives you more time to get used to your astral surroundings and execute your plan with no pressure at all.

Chapter Three: What to Expect

So, you want to go on an astral adventure. Well, it's only fitting that you should know what you're getting into and what to expect on your journey.

Vibrations

Most experienced astral projectors can tell you about the vibrations. When it's your first time experiencing them, they can feel quite disturbing. As I described before, it feels like you're being electrocuted, but there's no pain. The vibrations are simply very intense when they come. When you start to feel the vibrations, it's best to allow them to do their thing and keep your mind as calm as possible.

Some people erroneously assume that the vibrations are what cause projection. That sensation is simply a byproduct of what's going on within you on an energetic level as you stir up your astral body. During the vibratory stage of astral projection, anyone observing you would see that your physical body looks perfectly fine and isn't vibrating at all, despite what you're feeling.

Sometimes, you may get the sense that the vibration is only happening in specific parts of your body. This means that your astral body is being formed in these parts. You may feel that they're floating outside of your regular body. This is nothing to be alarmed about. This happens because those are the parts of your body that are completely relaxed and free of tension. If you carry tension in any part of your body, you may find your astral body stuck at that point when you try to leave. This is why a deep relaxation technique should be employed before you try to exit your body.

Distortion of Physics

There are some planes where the astral world seems to mimic the physics of the physical one completely, but this isn't always the case. Most of the time, you'll notice things are very odd. You could hold your cellphone, or at least the astral copy of it, and wonder why it feels as light as a piece of paper. You could walk and feel your feet are both off the floor for several seconds longer than usual.

You can walk through walls, drop through the floor, jump through the ceiling. You can make it to outer space in three seconds flat. The rules of the physical world go entirely out the window.

Mind Split

You may notice a feeling of bilocation or duality, where it's like you're in two different bodies at once. But, of course, your consciousness is limitless, so it's not such a stretch to entertain the fact that you really can be in two places (at least!) at the same time.

Your body isn't left as an empty shell when you switch your consciousness to the astral. Your consciousness is still there. So, while *Behind Her Eyes* (2021) was an excellent show, its suggestion that your body can be possessed by someone else is completely ludicrous and nothing for you to worry about.

This mind-split phenomenon has led to the assumption that such things as "astral watchers" and "sentinels" exist and require you to cast protection spells against them to stay safe. Unfortunately, many don't realize that you're always safe, and you have a silver cord that keeps you alive. It connects you to your body and can't be severed except when you die. So, there's no one watching and waiting to pounce on your "empty" body.

Get rid of the notion that your body is empty when you go exploring. You have to, because knowing this will help you get better at recalling your journeys. All you need to learn then is how to download the experiences you had in your astral form into your physical brain.

Fluctuations in Reality

As a new astral projector, you will have to contend with the fluctuations in reality when you've successfully left your body. One second, you're in your room, and the next, you're at the burger shop watching people order... cars.

A possible reason this happens is a lack of control over the mind. Most people are always thinking. You can probably relate to having steady chatter going through your head, day in and day out. You may see something or someone that causes you to think a thought in the astral realm, and that thought manifests before you, adding to the fluctuation. Your subconscious mind demonstrates its power before your very eyes. This portion of your mind is capable of creating the most intricate and impressive of worlds in a matter of seconds. If you're full of fear, then you can bet your subconscious will generate scenarios that will make you call out for your mother.

I'm Melting!

Whenever you try to take a close look at your astral body parts when you're out and about, you will notice that they melt in a matter of seconds. This is especially true when it comes to the hands. Look away, and it all feels nice and solid, but look again, and you'll notice you're getting stretchy and melting away. Likewise, your fingers can look ridiculously long, or you may have too many of them. Don't worry about any of this. If it bothers you, look away and look back, and they should be okay again. The intriguing thing is that nothing else you look at will melt away as you observe it—just you.

While we're on the subject of hands, if you ever find that your environment is too unstable, all you have to do is look at your hands. For some reason, this will send a little shock wave from the astral body to the physical. This helps keep the fluctuations in check and stops you from forgetting you're projecting.

All Here, All Now

Don't be surprised if you find yourself in a different period on Earth, whether past or future. Of course, it all exists now, but we experience linear time and not simultaneous time because we live in a world of time and space.

You can drop in on the lives of your past and future selves, as well as all other alternate selves that exist. It's a fascinating way to explore choices you may want to make for yourself in your actual life that you may never have considered if you hadn't dropped in on your other lives.

Astral Projection Stories

Leaving My Body the First Time

After being plagued by the memory of my spontaneous projection, I finally decided to look into what had happened to me. I was blown away. Then when I discovered that this was something I could deliberately induce, I just knew I had to try. I recall a long time before I had that experience, some kid at school talked about people being able to leave their bodies and travel the world. I'd thought she was full of it, but it turns out I was wrong.

When I discovered that astral projection could be deliberately induced, I had already been learning about lucid dreaming for months and making a point of keeping a dream journal, doing reality checks, and so on. So, I figured it couldn't be that hard. Intuitively, I knew I'd be able to leave on purpose this time.

I lay down and took a nap while intending to leave my body and do my best to keep my mind alert. The next thing I knew, I began to feel intense vibrations coursing through my body. The vibrations were so severe that it felt like I was being electrocuted, but in a way that felt pleasant and grew more and more enjoyable as I relaxed into it. I couldn't believe it. What was going on?

Next, I willed my astral body to leave my physical one. At first, it was a bit difficult. Imagine pulling gum out of your hair. That's how it felt, except my astral body was the gum, and my physical one just didn't seem to want to let go.

Eventually, I came out of my body and looked around the room. I didn't look at my body because I'd read that I shouldn't do that, or I'd get sucked back in. So I took a few steps toward the door, but then I had to stop because I was suddenly hit with the realization that there's no such thing as death or the finality of it as we think of it.

I realized that who we really are is so much more. We're immortal! I also realized that life really is just a game. It's real, alright, but we take it far too seriously so that we've forgotten the eternal beings we are. These realizations hit me all at once like a thought block was downloaded into my mind.

With that, I returned to my body. It was as though an intelligence had informed me telepathically that that was enough for one session. Since that experience, I've grown bolder in life, lost all fear of death, and I have pleasant psychic experiences every day. This singular experience helped me get rid of my depression and anxiety as well.

Projecting at Age Seven

Katy's favorite way to astral project is through lucid dreams. When she first decided to project, she would keep trying to get out of her body, but she failed. So, she chose to learn lucid dreaming, doing her best to recall her dreams, so she could tell what the dream signs were. Those dream signs would alert her to the fact that she was dreaming and help her achieve lucidity.

Soon, she successfully projected from a dream. As soon as she realized she was lucid, she generated a falling sensation within herself to turn the lucid dream into an astral projection. The next thing she knew, she went from being in the park to being right back in her bedroom—except she wasn't in bed. Instead, she was looking at herself in bed.

She watched as her physical body stirred, and within her, she felt odd. It was like the physical her was aware of being watched and was feeling a bit of fear. Then, intuitively, she decided to communicate to her physical self that all was well. At that moment, she felt herself both standing next to the bed *and* lying on it as well. Then, unable to contain her excitement at the sensation of being more than one person, she found herself back in her body, awake.

Launched into Outer Space

I lay still in bed, allowing the vibrations to wash over me, waiting until it all evened out nicely. Then, I rolled out of my body and immediately headed out the door, desperate to get away from my sleeping form, so I didn't get sucked right back in.

It was night when I headed out. The sky was full of stars, a lot clearer and more beautiful than in my normal waking life, where the city's lights make the night sky a tad harder to appreciate. I thought about hovering, not too high because I had a fear of heights at the time, but just high enough to look down on the rooftops in my neighborhood and journey on from there.

I gave the floor a light tap with my right foot, and the next thing I knew, I was launched up and off the floor just like a rocket! The speed was intense. The fact that the ground, then my neighborhood, then the entire Earth was rapidly receding almost sent me into a panic. To bring some calm to my mind, I held on to my wrist and pressed down hard. Then I came to a stop.

Just then, I looked around, and there was the most breathtaking view I'd ever seen in my whole life. There were all sorts of stars, planets, moons, and other debris. It looked nothing like the universe I'd seen in textbooks, on TV, and the internet. Everything was pulsing with a certain glow. The planets here had beautiful colors that I cannot describe because they have no Earthly equivalent for me to relate them to. Then, I got a thought block that made it clear I had traveled beyond the known universe.

I had a feeling of oneness with it all, a sense of peace, of being a fuller version of myself. This was incredibly humbling, in a good way. I burst into tears because I couldn't stand how beautiful it all was. The soundless sound I heard drove me to levels of ecstasy, when I worried I would soon burst and become part of the debris. Unable to keep my emotions in check, I woke up in my room to find my cheeks damp with tears and my heart filled with homesickness. The words left my mouth before their meaning hit me: "I want to go back home."

Helping From a Distance

Brandon's dad was admitted to the hospital for COVID-19. For weeks, no one was allowed to visit him. Then, things took a turn for the worst when he got bilateral pneumonia and had a stroke on top of that. Brandon's father was in a very critical condition, battling for his life.

Brandon then began to visit his father via the astral plane each night, so he wouldn't be alone through that difficult period. When Brandon realized his dad could see him, Brandon telepathically encouraged him to stay strong and hold on. He shared thoughts of love and support and let him know the entire family and all their friends were thinking about him, praying for him, hoping to be able to visit someday soon.

Eventually, Brandon's dad was allowed to have guests, and his mother and sister were the first to visit. Brandon's sister called to let him know that their father had just told her Brandon had been visiting every night the whole time. He mentioned that he had seen Brandon usually between 3 am to 5 am. His mother thought he was insane, but his sister knew Brandon had always astral projected and reminded her of this.

Brandon's dad passed on a message to him to please ask the nurse to keep it down on his next visit so he could get some sleep. So, on his next astral visit, Brandon sent a message to the nurses via telepathy, asking them to keep it down. In response, one of the nurses went over to where Brandon's dad was and shut his door so the noise wouldn't bother him. So finally, Brandon went to visit his dad in the flesh, and his dad thanked him for helping out with the nurses, as he was able to get a good night's sleep at last.

A Peek into One of My Lives

After a session of exploring, I intended to head back to my body and record my experiences. Instead, I found myself in the body of a Roman soldier. I could tell right away that this was me in a past life, while retaining consciousness of my present life. I had a brief moment of amusement when I realized my chest was flatter than it should be, and I had all this muscle and strength.

The amusement quickly passed when I took in the scene before me. It was horrific. Bloody. I could feel myself as both my present self and the Roman soldier, who I realized was a legatus—a high-ranking Roman officer. The old me watched with a cold sort of enjoyment as my men butchered what was left of the enemy, relishing the sound of metal slicing flesh, of men begging for their lives. The present me felt very sick and disgusted with it all. I began to feel a very uncomfortable energy, almost like an electrical force field that wanted to get me out of the man's body. I gladly allowed myself to get out of there and woke up, thankfully in my own room again.

Part Two: Getting Ready for the Astral Plane

Chapter Four: Overcome Your Mind's Limitations

Your mind can either be your best ally or your worst enemy. It's a neutral tool, simply waiting for you to program in commands for it to follow. Chances are, you have already established patterns of thought when it comes to spirituality. If those thoughts serve you, then that's great. It means you're halfway to success with leaving your body already.

Suppose those thoughts are full of superstition about nonexistent evil, or they are all misconceptions about phenomena outside the physical realm that suggest you're a powerless, helpless victim. In that case, that's not going to bode well for you. You might not even be able to leave your body to begin with. So, let's talk more about the mind and how to make it work for you, instead of against you.

Your Mind as a Barrier

Some say you need to figure out your subconscious thoughts and beliefs before finally achieving your dreams. This school of thought suggests that those beliefs remain hidden until we slave night and day through hypnosis and therapy to get them out in the open.

While it is true that the subconscious is powerful, this power needs to be channeled through your conscious mind, which you *do* have control over. For example, suppose your subconscious mind coughs up a thought about how you'll "never" be able to astral project. It's left to you to deliberately use your conscious mind to either accept that belief or replace it with a preferred one in the most nonjudgmental way that you can. Then your subconscious will begin to work with the new idea. When you feel or think something to the contrary, your job is to gently, lovingly remind yourself, your subconscious, of the new belief you have chosen. That's all there is to it.

Here's where I'm going with this: if there's even a bit of you that strongly feels you should *not* leave your body, you're going to have a hard time exiting, let alone exploring that wonderful plane. However, since you cannot go rooting about your subconscious to find the disempowering beliefs, you can try a better way to get your head in the game.

First, you must decide that you're the kind of person who always astral projects. Decide that this is who you are, that astral projection is easy, always has been, and always will be. Sure, you may be just starting out. Still, you should begin by assuming the mindset of a professional *who is always willing to learn something new and get better.* That last bit is critical because if you believe you've mastered all you need to know, you leave yourself no room for growth. You will become too proud to consider trying new methods that may work out well for you in the end.

Once you have decided you're this person, the next thing to do is *ask yourself what this version of you would think about this hang-up you have about astral travel.* When you do this, you will notice that you begin to come up with convincing reasons your fears are unfounded. You develop the courage and mind control you need in order to learn for yourself what it's like in the other realm.

Before you begin, accept that this is unfamiliar territory for you. Therefore, you will encounter the novel and the strange—and that's okay. However, if you experience any unpleasantness, don't shut it down out of fear. Instead, become curious about what you experienced, why it happened, and how you can handle it better the next time around.

If you let fear take over and make you shut down, then you have allowed your mind to become a barrier to your success. Remember, the mind is a tool given to you by the source to serve you. When you have an experience that scares you, and you shy away from it, it's the same thing as refusing to use a hammer because it dropped on your little toe that one time. Do you say to yourself, "I'm never going to touch a hammer for as long as I live?" Of course not. What you do is suck it up, pick it up, and mindfully use the tool with a firmer grip on it.

Mind as the Channel to the Astral Plane

Laws govern all planes of existence, and the astral realm is no exception. You interact with these laws with your mind. Even before you move your physical body, you first have that experience of movement in your mind.

Thankfully, you know the right way to reach for a bottle of water. Maybe as a kid, you were clumsier about it. Perhaps you'd knock the glass around a bit and send water sloshing over its sides. However, with time, working with your mind, you mastered proper motor control. Now you know how to move your hand to pick up the glass without incident. The same thing applies to using your mind to master any skill or learn something new, including the art of astral travel.

In the astral planes, the law of attraction (which states that "like attracts like") reigns supreme. You may think that sentence is a New Age scam, but that is the way life works, and you see this law manifest even faster on planes higher than this physical one. This is one more reason your mind can be a barrier to your success with soul travel. If you think you can't, then you're right. If you assume that you will succeed and that this is easy for you, you're also right.

You will find that everything is very fluid on the astral plane, very responsive to intention and thought. So, the principle of like attracting like works incredibly fast here, almost in an instant. If you have a fear that there's something sinister, terrifying, or malevolent that's out to get you, that's what will happen. However, if you calm down and use your mind to intend and realize you are safe, you are loved, and drawn only to high vibrations, then you will meet entities who resonate with what you're putting out there. You'll find them to be full of love and kindness and very willing and eager to help you. In other words, your tribe depends on your vibe.

Take charge of your mind. Understand that whatever you focus on will be magnified by *a lot*. Suppose the assumption you hold of yourself is that you're a victim, subject to the whims and caprices of whoever and whatever. In that case, you're going to create situations where you get to be the victim. You'll attract the entities who will help you embody that assumption—which is *not* what you want.

A healthy mindset to have is that you're immortal, powerful, and spiritual. You're a part of the Divine Spark itself, which means you have no end, and you cannot be hurt. You are a part of the Source, masquerading as human, having a fun adventure being an Earthling. That's it. Since you are the Source itself, you have all the energy, power, and ability you need to remain safe from whatever life throws your way.

Healthy Mindset for Astral Travel

First, treat other entities the way you'd rather be treated. Next, treat others the way they'd rather be treated. This may sound like a paradox, but it is not. The point is that you should accept the existence of all other entities as valid, understand that they are sovereign, and have their own free will. As long as they aren't forcing their will on you, you should offer them the same courtesy.

Understand that there are always limits to deal with when you're in the astral realm. There are exceptions to everything. For instance, I once found myself in a very solid zone where there was absolutely nothing I could manipulate with my mind. I couldn't walk through walls like I used to. This was new to me after many years of journeying in the astral.

Speaking of exceptions, just because you have preconceived notions about what good or evil should look like doesn't mean your first assumption about an entity is valid. Thankfully, this is a plane that engages your feelings. So, trust your intuition when you're dealing with people in the astral realm. Frankly, this is a healthy mindset to have in your waking world as well.

Fear often is a result of ignorance. By default, people fear what they don't understand. It takes a genuinely conscious person to become curious about their fears so that they can surmount them and grow even more enlightened. Having said that, I would like to address some misconceptions about astral travel so that you know you have nothing to worry about.

Clearing Up Misconceptions

Astral projection is not dangerous. You astral project every night. You just aren't aware of it, and you haven't mastered how to recall your explorations just yet. It's about as dangerous as sleeping. The difference is that you choose to become aware of what you get up to when you hit the hay.

Sleep paralysis is a natural phenomenon. There's no "demon sitting on your chest." It's a natural thing that happens to you every night, with the only difference being you caught your body doing it this time.

Your physical body is not empty and waiting to be possessed by a demon. Again, your body has its own consciousness. There's no way any being could oust you from your own body. As you project, you send out a copy of your energy body to explore the realm. You exist in multiple dimensions, always, all the time.

You will not die from astral projecting. If anyone passes on while outside the body, it's due to a preexisting medical condition or something else. You cannot die from exploring consciousness. So, don't believe the horror stories.

Every astral projector is protected all the time. You don't have to worry about someone severing your silver cord, causing you to die as you project. We all have guides and our Higher Selves who look after us. These beings are mighty and will make sure to keep you safe from all harm. Also, you would be wise just to assume you're always safe and loved. This way, you will have nothing to be protected from.

You can never get so far away from your body that you have trouble returning to it. You are connected to your Earth body by your silver cord. You may or may not see the cord, but it is there, and it only ever breaks when you die in the physical realm.

To get back to your body faster, you can simply shut your eyes and think about your body on the bed. Then, feel yourself on the bed, and you will be teleported there right away. Also, know that if your physical body experiences any disturbances, from noise to the need to pee, you will wake up right away, whether you want to or not.

Consciously Releasing Mental Blocks

If you're finding it difficult to access the astral plane, you may have mental blocks to contend with. You, like everyone else, may have assumed that all your thoughts are true, and some of those thoughts may be counterproductive to successful astral trips. The statement

"I think; therefore, I am" is cute but detrimental. Instead, it should be, "I Am; therefore I Am." Everything else that seeks to define "I Am" or consciousness puts a limit on your naturally abundant, limitless nature.

The best way to reprogram your mind to give you the thoughts you would like is first to understand that **all thoughts are neutral until you give them life by assuming they are true.** Then, know that you're constantly deciding what is true for you at every given moment. Even when you're not deciding, that's simply you deciding not to decide! So, you may as well deliberately choose that your preferred, empowering thoughts are true for you.

Addicted to Thinking

Lose your addiction to thinking and thoughts. Thoughts run over and over on a loop. Little wonder most people just accept them as being their own, when really, it's just the monkey mind looking for stuff to do. So, here's how to calm the monkey in your head.

1. First, find somewhere comfortable where you can sit comfortably in an upright position. You may also lie down if you're sure you won't fall asleep. Make sure you're wearing loose, comfy clothing and that you won't be bothered or distracted for at least ten minutes, fifteen tops.

2. Next, shut your eyes and slightly part your lips.

3. Breathe in through your nose. Make it a loving, generous breath. Allow your awareness to map the path of your inhale.

4. Exhale through your slightly parted lips, following the breath with your awareness.

5. Repeat this cycle over and over until you notice your breathing and thinking slowing down. Your body will relax, deeper and deeper.

6. Place your awareness on your heart chakra, which is just in between the lungs. Just sit with your attention on that energy center. Relax with it.

7. Notice when the next thought comes into your mind. Notice the way it emerges while still keeping your awareness on the heart chakra. It doesn't matter if the idea is negative, positive, or neutral. Don't care about what it means. Just notice how it comes up and where it comes from.

8. See if you can notice the space in between your thoughts. Also, notice the space each thought emerged from.

9. With your awareness still on your heart center, observe whether you're thinking. Observe if you're the thinker of those thoughts, or simply the observer, watching as they come. Notice how you didn't bring them up, but they showed up on their own. Notice the itch the mind feels to latch onto them but be gentle and without judgment as you do so. Keep your awareness on the love flowing from your heart center as you notice the space these thoughts come from.

This is an exercise you shouldn't rush through. Also, the more you do this, the deeper the insights you will glean. The more detached you will be from your thoughts, which is good since you're allowing the negative thoughts to fly back to wherever they came from. This is a good practice for peace in your life.

Open Your Mind

We've mastered the science of journeying into outer space. It's time to master the journey into "inner space." This is a vital thing for all of humanity to do, as the awareness of our true nature will sort out many of the problems we face today. However, the trouble is you can't master consciousness if you don't even want to keep an open mind.

The correct attitude to adopt is that of a kid learning to write their alphabets. When you were young, you could have argued that there's no reason a squiggly line should give you the "s" sound and that there's no reason it has to be written that way, either. However, you didn't do that. Instead, you learned every letter, and you learned to read and write each one. Then you learned to combine them all. Now you have access to amazing information from books because you *chose* to keep an open mind and understand what the adults were fussing about.

Keep this same energy when it comes to astral projection. Staying open means you get to learn new things, and you grow thanks to your explorations in consciousness. Staying open is how you keep your body and soul burning with passion and joy. It's how you find more and more aspects of yourself that you didn't know about. The goal of life is continuous expansion, which leads to joy, which leads to further growth. So, stay open! Get curious. Knowing what you know now, aren't you interested in learning about all of your lives?

Curiosity never killed the cat. It just made it realize it had more than nine lives—just like you do.

Chapter Five: Your Dream Journal

Keeping a journal is a potent practice that can help you see how far you've come in all areas of life. In the same vein, you should regularly record your dreams so that you can notice patterns and themes that pop up in them over time and grow in awareness. They are a treasure trove of information that can help you with the relationships, problems, and activities you engage in within your waking world.

Benefits of a Dream Journal

Stress Reduction

Journaling is a great way to review things you may have chosen to suppress instead of dealing with them. The stuff we hide can add to our stress in ways we may not be able to detect otherwise. When we sleep, a lot of what goes on in our dreams reflects our waking lives. So, writing down your dreams will help you notice what patterns show up and help you figure out what you may need to pay attention to in your physical life so you can fix it.

Increased Creativity

The more you write down your dreams, the more you'll engage your creative side, which is strongly connected to dreaming. The easier it will become for you to create new ideas and thoughts—a bonus if you work in a field that calls for right-brain thinking.

Improved Dream Recall

Let's face it. You're reading this book because you want to experience more of the other world consciously. Other waking life benefits are just extra perks. So, when you write your dreams down, your dream recall improves. This works because the process of remembering your dreams and noting them down signals to your mind that your dreams are important to you. As a result, you'll be able to remember more and more. With time, you'll find you can recall every little detail in your dreams, and this will be of immense benefit to you when you begin your astral visits.

Boost in Dream Lucidity

Recording every dream you have will cause you to notice the things that usually happen over and over in your dreams. In addition, it helps you to recognize the oddities that make dreams a distinctly different experience from waking life. Those oddities are called dream signs. The next time you see them in a dream, you will be triggered awake.

Boost in Logical Thought

Journaling also helps you to be better with left-brain, analytical thinking. For example, to realize you're in a dream, you need the rational part of you to spot the clues and dead giveaways that let you know there's something off about the world you're in. The wonderful thing is that you'll experience this boost in rational thinking in your waking life as well. For instance, you can tell when things aren't adding up. You can also think your way through any issue when everyone else is losing their minds around you. You know how to remain calm and rational when tempers are flying, so you're the one person in the room who doesn't leap to irrational conclusions and take regrettable actions.

How does this help you with astral projection? For one thing, you can convert your lucid dream into an astral projection with the correct technique. For another, you will get better at avoiding *false awakenings.*

When you travel to the astral realm's *real-time zone* (where everything closely matches your physical environment), you may mistakenly assume you are awake. Ever had a moment when you woke up, did everything you had to do for the day, and then woke up **again** to find you dreamed it all? That's an instance of false awakening.

Improved Emotional Intelligence

When you note your dreams down, you connect with your emotions better. This is because recalling and writing them will inevitably evoke feelings that you will naturally pay attention to, so you can find out why you feel the way you do.

Noting your dreams will also help you learn why it's just as important to be in charge of your mind in waking life as well as waking dreams or projections. When you choose to watch a horror flick or something sad before bed, you will notice how that colors your dreams. When you fall asleep in high spirits, you will also see that translate into your dreams. Also, you'll notice how the emotions from a dream color your morning and possibly the rest of your day. You'll be more conscious about acknowledging and sorting out your feelings. This alone will drastically improve the quality of your life.

Better Control in Dreams and Astral Projections

The more you write down your dreams, the better you'll get at manipulating everything that happens in that realm. If you're the sort of person who has to deal with poor sleep on account of constant nightmares, it should be immediately evident to you how amazing this is. Rather than give in to the fear, you can realize you're dreaming and influence the dream. For example, you could neutralize whatever is causing your fear or make it smaller than you. Or you could turn it into something hilarious, change the environment, or simply choose to end it.

Creative Problem-Solving

Any experienced lucid dreamer or astral projector can tell you many stories about how they came up with creative solutions to problems that seemed impossible to fix.

We live in a world that so desperately cleaves to logic, refusing to rock the boat, always sticking to tradition and the status quo. The beautiful thing about the astral realm is that all of those rules and conventions are tossed out the window. What this means for you is boundless, limitless creativity. You can use your dreamscape to fix a problem by intending to receive an answer in your dreams and trusting you'll understand it when you get it. As soon as you do, make sure to write the answer down.

Tips for Keeping a Dream Journal

1. **Summarize with single words.** If you wake up in the middle of the night and you're much too tired to whip out your notebook or phone to journal in your app, then consider just writing down a few words to summarize. Then, in the morning, you can fill in the rest of it. For instance, say you had a dream about being one of the Von Trapp children. You were singing and dancing on a hill with Fraulein Maria while a disapproving nun chased you all around. In that case, you could write: "Hill. Nun. Music. Von Trapp." This should be enough to jog your memory so you can fill in the details in the morning.

2. Be generous with details. You'll get better at noticing details the more you journal, but even if you're just starting out, do your best to note the minutiae of what you experienced or saw. Recall what time of day it was, who was with you, what you could hear, colors, sensations, and emotions. Don't be hard on yourself if you notice you're not noticing enough. Just intend that you will, and over time, that will improve. It's a worthy goal, too, because you'll be better at interpreting your dreams and won't have to rely on blogs to tell you what your dreams mean (a pointless thing to do since dreams are highly subjective).

3. Draw your dream if it's easier. If you're better at expressing yourself in pictures than words, then it's okay to draw your dreams. You'll capture a lot more that you might have missed had you tried to write. On the other hand, if you can express yourself in both words and pictures, that is awesome, and you should do that. You'll be even better at correctly interpreting your dreams.

4. Not a dreamer? Here's what you should do. First, write down how you feel when you wake up. Some people argue that they never dream. What's really going on is they *don't remember* dreaming. Everyone exists multi-dimensionally. We're not always focused on Earth all the time, so not all your nights will be dreamless. To fix this, just note down how you feel, and trust that very soon, you'll begin to get more details on your dreams. Don't beat yourself up over not knowing anything more than your emotions, or else you'll slow the process down.

5. Contrast your waking life with your dreams. You want to note down what your day was like and notice your final thoughts before turning in for the night. You should also pay attention to whatever you consumed mentally, whether it was a book, an article, a YouTube video, whatever. After writing your dream, the next step is to look back on what you experienced the day before the dream and see if you can find clues about why you had the dream you did. You can also use your dream to analyze how your new day goes and see if you can find any connections between the two.

6. Be on the lookout for patterns. Over a number of dreams, you may begin to notice a pattern unfold. For example, you may find you're constantly dreaming of a specific place, or you consistently see cats. Maybe it's someone who's always in your dreams, or the same sort of event plays out but in different locations. These patterns can lead you to issues you need to deal with in the waking world that you've been suppressing, and you can even find the solution within them as well. So, don't just write your dreams and toss your journal aside. Instead, always review it for clues. A good journal app will allow you to search for specific keywords, so you can tell if something pops up often enough for you to call it a pattern.

How to Keep a Dream Journal

You could just write the date you had your dream and its details, but ideally, noting other elements can help you learn more about yourself and your dream habits.

What kind of dream journal to use: This is primarily up to you. If you want to go old-school because you love the feel of pen and paper, then you can get a notepad. You should only use this for your dreams and their connections to your waking life. Nothing more.

If you would prefer to use your phone, that's an option as well. Switch to dark mode or any other visual mode that won't cause you to wake up fully as you type in the keywords of your dreams. This will be of immense help to you, especially if you wake up in the middle of the night to record them.

There are lots of apps you can use. You could go for the classic EverNote, Penzu, or Google's Keep. You could check out your app store and search for "dream journal," go through the reviews to find one that suits you. Some of these dream journal apps even come with alerts to help you perform reality checks throughout your day, and they also remind you to write your dreams. A good app for this is Awoken. If you'd rather record your dreams in audio format, that's an option as well. You can use the recording app on your phone or pay for one that allows you to transcribe audio to text if you'd rather read your entries.

When to write: You don't want to write your dream down as soon as you wake up. If you immediately roll out and reach for your journal, you may forget some crucial bits. So first, remain there in bed for about a minute. Next, work your way backward in the sequence of dream events until there's nothing left to remember. Then you can write out the keywords to serve as a reminder as you note down the dream in more detail.

What should be in your journal?

- The day you had the dream.
- The time you went to bed and the time you woke up.
- Whether your sleep was interrupted.
- Whether you remember your dream in full or not.
- The time of day in your dream.
- The characters you saw: animal, human, or otherwise.
- The sequence of events in the dream.
- Physical sensations, if any.
- The emotions you feel.
- Your interpretation of the dream.

- Whether you astral traveled.

- The sequence of events in your astral projection.

Where to keep your journal? Ideally, you want it as close to your bed as possible. Get a bedside table if you don't have one. If it's not uncomfortable, you can keep your journal underneath your pillow.

Your Astral Journal

If you want, you can have a separate journal for recording your astral journeys alone. However, you might find it a lot more practical to simply record your astral projections in the same journal you use for your lucid dreams. All you'd have to do is make sure that they are clearly marked, so it's easier for you to get to what you want to read.

In your astral journal, include the following details:

1. Did you deliberately leave your physical body, or did you catch your astral body as it re-entered?

2. Was your re-entry deliberate or not?

3. What time did you project?

4. What method did you use to project?

5. Did you leave your body forcefully, or was it easy for you?

6. Was your exit easier or harder than the last time?

7. Was there anything you did differently in your routine that made it easier or harder?

8. Did you give in to the urge to roll over or scratch an itch?

9. Narrate your experiences during your trip.

10. What did you eat before leaving your body, if anything?

11. How soon after eating did you attempt to leave your body?

12. Were there any peculiar energy sensations you felt that were unusual for you during the vibratory state? Describe them.

13. Did you fully recollect your astral memories, or only partially?

14. Did you have a plan, and did you execute it successfully?

15. If you didn't execute it fully, write why.

This may seem like a little too much information to write down in your journal, but the more entries you make, the more likely it is that you will see a pattern emerge. In addition, all of this information will help you to know what you're doing right and what you need to fix.

So, with each new astral trip you make, you can correct your course along the way. Soon, you will find that you've gotten a lot of the technical stuff out of the way, so you can focus on enjoying your experiences. If you decide to share your experiences, you'll be adding tremendous value to the growing body of work on this topic, which will definitely help both neophyte and veteran travelers alike.

Finally, keeping track of all these variables will show you just how far you've come on your journey. In addition, tracking your progress will give you the encouragement and enthusiasm you need to continue with your explorations, creating a positive feedback loop that will accelerate your learning process.

Chapter Six: Developing Mindfulness

If you've been paying attention, you must have already figured out this topic was coming. You need to be a master of your mind to traverse the astral world. So, what better way to learn to tame the mind than practicing mindfulness?

Mindfulness Defined

Mindfulness is a practice that requires you to be completely aware of the here and now, without trying to interpret it, or judge it, or label it. There are so many ways to practice this art of living in the moment. There's meditation with or without guided imagery and breathing methods to place your full attention on the breath. These practices have the added benefit of helping you to de-stress in body and mind. The more relaxed you are, the deeper the levels of awareness you can reach.

This is a practice that has heaps of benefits when it comes to astral projection. The ability to remain nonjudgmental in a given place and time will automatically deepen your focus regardless of what's happening. You'll pick up on details better and get whatever messages you need to help you along life's journey.

Remaining in the moment also means you'll have fewer fluctuations to deal with when you're having a lucid dream or astral projection. Since the astral realm is susceptible to your thoughts, developing mindfulness will help you be more deliberate about what you entertain in your head. You will only give energy to the ideas that give you the results you seek.

Benefits of Mindfulness

Stress reduction: this world is a high-octane one. You may not be shooting monsters or bad guys in an action movie, but chances are you're experiencing the same levels of stress anyone would in those situations. Inevitably, we have recurring negative feelings and thoughts, which further feed the pain, depression, stress, and anxiety already caused by stressful situations. Whether it's finances, health issues, or the state of the nation, these things can translate into insomnia, hypertension, and other health problems you really don't want to have to deal with.

One way to mitigate the damaging effects of these stressful times is through practicing mindfulness. When you choose to be mindful, you will find it's easier for you to accept where you are. When you no longer fight a circumstance or situation, you take away its power over your life. You put yourself in a position to see the neon exit signs clearly to escape those issues.

Improved focus and awareness: if you've always had trouble focusing, whether because of a health issue or just a lack of discipline, mindfulness will help you in spades. Your attention span will grow with practice. Soon, you'll find you're able to give your attention to single tasks for extended periods without feeling the need to look at cat videos on Facebook or something else equally distracting.

Reduction in burnout: burnout, at its core, is the exhaustion you feel when you no longer want to deal with a particularly persistent situation; have refused to accept it or to look for ways to turn it into a positive; and either can't or won't let the problematic issue go.

Practicing mindfulness puts you in touch with your emotions, allowing you to know when to persist with a problem or take a break and come back to it later without beating yourself up. With practice, you'll also find that you're able to be a part of that situation with no judgment and no push-back on your end. This allows you to find the joy in it if you want to or to energetically disconnect from it. This disconnection will set up a chain of events where you finally have the perfect solution to this persistent issue, or the problem resolves itself on its own.

Better sleep: with better control over your mind, you'll find it easier to go to bed, since you won't be bothered by stray thoughts like whether cows can swim. You can set an intention to fall asleep quickly and easily and experience precisely that. With mastery of mind, you know what it means not to give energy to your thoughts. You understand that your mind is not unlike a generator that's been running all day. You've turned it off, and it's still a bit hot, but you don't worry about it because you know it's off, and so it has no choice but to cool down.

Mindfulness and Astral Projection

Make a habit of practicing mindfulness in waking life. You'll find it's a lot easier for you to project successfully. When you're concentrating on being right here, right now, you'll see that this habit spills over to your astral projections too. You'll also find that you're constantly achieving lucidity when you dream. You'll catch yourself just as you're about to leave your body, even when you didn't plan to.

When you look at your hands in your dreams or projections, the entire world stabilizes. This happens because your attention becomes rooted in the moment. However, you don't want to spend the whole time just looking at your hands because you're afraid you'll come out of it. This is why you should take up mindfulness and make it a habit.

Without mindfulness, you'll find that your mind wanders way too much. You might assume this means you should wind up in interesting places during your astral projection, but it's not like that. Instead, you'll find yourself losing lucidity. You'll forget you're in the astral realm and go back to your uncritical way of thinking during dreams. You'll forget your experiences, so you can't even journal them when you get back. Also, you'll find yourself constantly experiencing false awakenings. I can tell you for a fact that it is pretty irritating to wake up and discover what you had assumed was waking life was the real-time zone.

When you've trained yourself to be mindful, you'll catch these false awakenings easily. For example, you may get out of bed to prepare for work and notice something out of place in your room. You'll also see how you feel a little different in your body than usual, and then it will hit you that you're projecting. The reason you'll notice is that you've made a habit of being fully here and now, so details don't escape you. Then you can choose to leave the real-time zone and go to higher levels of the astral plane.

Mindfulness Exercises

Awareness of the Present

1. Find a comfortable and quiet place where you can sit. If there are others around you, ask that you be left alone for just ten to fifteen minutes.

2. Wearing loose clothing, sit in a comfortable position. You don't have to sit in a lotus position if it hurts your knees or isn't your style. The goal is to feel as natural as you can.

3. Simply observe the moment. Don't try to silence your mind or force yourself to be calm. Just be. Notice the moment, and don't judge it.

4. When you notice yourself judging or giving the things you see around you and feel within you any meaning, just notice that and then allow the judgment to pass. Let your mind gently return to the moment, just the way it is, label-free.

5. Repeat this process of returning your mind to the present each time you notice it's back to judging, labeling, giving meaning to things. Do so lovingly. Don't judge yourself, no matter how many times you've found yourself carried away from the moment.

This exercise is a simple one, but simple doesn't mean it's easy. Don't let that scare you away. Perfection is not the goal here. Instead, you should thank yourself for noticing your mind's gone off on a tangent, to begin with, because that means you're getting better at being mindful.

Follow the Breath Meditation

1. Go somewhere peaceful and quiet. Get rid of all distractions for ten to fifteen minutes.

2. In loose and comfy clothing, sit down. You may be on the floor or in a chair, whatever works for you.

3. Keep your body relaxed and in good posture, with your spine upright. If this feels uncomfortable, adjust your body till you feel good. You may keep your hands on your thighs in whatever way feels comfortable. There should be no straining.

4. Shut your eyes and slightly part your lips.

5. Take in a deep breath through your nose. Observe its sound and the path it takes as it moves through your nostrils, filling your belly and lungs.

6. Hold that breath for a second or two, paying attention to the feeling within you as it waits for release.

7. Next, exhale through your slightly parted lips. You might notice that your exhale takes longer than your inhale. This is normal. Observe the breath as it flows out of your belly and lungs, through your nostrils. Notice the very point where the breath loses touch with your body.

8. If your mind wanders—and chances are it will—notice that, with no judgment, and then with love and appreciation for yourself, return your attention to your breath. Do this no matter how many times your mind wanders, never judging yourself, being kind to yourself no matter what.

9. Repeat this process until the time elapses. Do this daily.

Tips for Remaining Mindful

Observe your emotions from a relaxed, detached point of view. Whether it's joy or anger or sadness, no matter what you're feeling, pay attention to the emotion without letting it consume you. Think of it like standing on the outside, looking in on yourself. First, there's the observer, and then there's the observed. Of course, you are both, but you can mindfully switch your awareness to being the observer at any given point in time. The more you do this, the more you'll grow in mindfulness.

Use positive affirmations. When you find yourself caught in a whirlwind of negativity, you can find your center using affirmations. To be clear, it's not about the words but the meaning and feeling behind the words with which you resonate. There's no power in words on their own. So, you should always use your affirmations positively and in the present.

Incorrect: I will **not** let this situation bring me down.

Correct: I am greater than this.

Incorrect: I am going to be excellent at astral projection.

Correct: I am an excellent astral projector.

Journal your life passively. In a separate journal, practice writing about your day with no judgment. Imagine you were peeking in on your life as someone else. The more you write about your life passively, the better you'll get at noticing your emotions, as well as your thoughts.

Make a point of really listening to people. When you're listening, really be there. Don't fiddle with your phone or your hands. Don't try to anticipate where they're going with what they're saying. Make no judgments about what you hear from them either. When you listen mindfully, you also notice that you're not preparing what to say in response. You're just in the moment.

Look with no judgment. Just as you listen, you can also look at people (and objects or places) without judgment. This is not the time to think, "Oh, they're so beautiful!" or "Wow, that's an ugly piece of art." Just look with no judgment. You can make eye contact and then allow your eyes to drift around their face as well, just taking it all in.

Mind your mind. Every now and then, just check in with your mind to see what's going on in there. Don't ask the question, "What am I thinking about?" because then you're giving yourself a mental wedgie. Your mind can answer back, "Well, now I'm thinking about what I'm thinking about!" Instead, what you want to do is just peek in from a detached perspective. Just notice what's going on in there. Don't try to notice by actively looking into your mind, but simply being in the moment and allowing it to roam. Imagine, if you will, that you're a house with open windows, while the thoughts that fly in and out are birds. You're stable, ever-present, while the birds flit in and out.

Make a habit of working out. When you're exercising at a decent intensity, you're forced to bring your entire focus to the moment. At the moment, your lungs demand air. Your muscles require energy. Your willpower demands that you push one second longer, go one rep further. All of these put together force you to be entirely in the here and now.

The workout must be hard enough to force you to have to focus (but not make you want to quit) because working out means you have to breathe, and there's nothing that grounds you in the present like the breath. It's the reason breathwork is so powerful and vital when it comes to the practice of mindfulness.

Set recurring alarms. When they go off, you can take just a minute, maybe five, to just be in the moment if you weren't before. Another way you can use this to empower yourself is to create a statement about you being the kind of person you want to be. Then, when the alarm goes off, for just a few minutes, see through your eyes, live through your body, and notice everything from the state of mind that the ideal version of yourself would.

You could also imagine that you *are* in an astral projection, and you just realized it thanks to the alarm. Then, what you do next is make a decision about doing something, and then do it. For example, you could decide to get up and stretch your legs, pick up the phone and call someone, or go look outside. No matter what action you choose, you're training yourself to be mindful during your projections. You're learning to follow through on your decisions with laser precision each time you're out of your body.

Turn off your phone. It's amazing how that tiny little rectangle takes us out of the moment every so often, with its incessant demand for our attention. It's not like it's just one thing you need to focus on when using your phone, either. Chances are, you have notifications from multiple apps.

Be deliberate about disconnecting yourself. Each day dedicate time to forget about emails, the media with its barrage of bad news, your overanxious mother's constant worrisome texts. Ignore all the notifications telling you that this challenge or that challenge demands you sink hours of your time scrolling through videos that are essentially the same. Instead, take that time and focus on being in the present, whether you just observe it or really get into a creative hobby like painting, creating something, immersing yourself in family time, or whatever else. Just unplug for a bit. It's a habit worth having and one you'll soon find hard to kick. You might feel antsy and have intense FOMO when you disconnect yourself from social media at first. Still, after a bit, you will notice you feel better than you have in a long time.

Chapter Seven: Astral Breathwork

I mentioned before that breath is vital when it comes to maintaining mindfulness. It's also essential for your astral travels. When you think about it, your breathing is so crucial that it isn't just your conscious mind in control. You fall asleep, and your lungs keep on trucking. Imagine being completely in charge of your breathing while having zero control over your mind. That's a scary thought. Just as the breath is essential for keeping your physical body going, it also helps with your astral one.

Breath-Work Defined

Breath-work refers to all breathing exercises designed to improve physical, mental, and spiritual health. It's about breathing intentionally. Practicing this often leads to better focus, more profound relaxation, and boundless energy when you need it.

Your job is to just breathe with breath-work, allowing whatever comes up in your mind to move on with no resistance. Conscious breathing leads to hypo-oxygenated cells, which means your blood has a lot of oxygen to work with, and your body can begin to heal at an accelerated rate. Your mind also benefits from the practice, healing what it needs to. It gets out of your way so that you can achieve more profound levels of meditation, more self-awareness, and a state of blissful surrender to the here and now.

Breathing and Stress

The next time you feel stressed, notice the way you're breathing. Typically, your breath will be shallow, ending in the upper chest. This means you're not getting as much air into your lungs as you should, and you're breathing faster than you should. Unfortunately, it's a sad truth that this is what most of us consider normal breathing.

Shallow breathing is closely connected to stress due to the sympathetic nervous system, also known as the SNS. This is the part of your autonomic nervous system in charge of your "fight, freeze, or flight" mechanism. When you're stressed, the SNS constricts your blood vessels. In turn, your heart rate goes up along with your respiration and blood pressure. Your digestive system also suffers.

Since the body and brain always influence one another, your body lets your brain know you're under stress through your shallow breathing. Your brain then sends your body information about how to act in response to the pressure, and that causes more shallow breathing and all the other harmful effects. This is why stress can seem like a rickety, never-ending roller coaster.

Your parasympathetic nervous system or PNS acts as a counterbalance to the SNS. It's your body's "rest and digest" system. What it does is help you to relax and feel calm. Just like the SNS, you can activate the PNS through your breathing. Take a moment to shut your eyes and imagine that you're somewhere that sets you at ease. You feel calm in this place. It's quiet and peaceful, and you just feel like relaxing there indefinitely. What you'll notice is that your breath is slower and deeper. That's because you feel more relaxed and are breathing with your diaphragm on account of that.

The deeper you breathe, the calmer your mind becomes, and the better you can direct it to do your bidding as it was designed to. Incorporating breath-work into your routine for mastering astral projection is an investment that will give back to you in spades.

Holotropic Breathwork

The etymology of the word "holotropic" is Greek, made up of the words *holos*, which means "whole," and *trepein*, which means "to move forward." Developed by Christina and Stanislav Grof, this breath-work technique is designed to help you feel like a whole person. With it, you can alter your state of consciousness without having to use drugs.

Also known as HB, it involves being in control of your breath, breathing faster than usual to affect your emotional, mental, and physical states of being. While this has a lot of therapeutic effects, it's usually used for spiritual purposes. You can use this breathing technique to grow awareness, which in turn will be helpful during your astral travel. When done right, you can use this to shift into higher states of consciousness. This, in turn, can trigger an awakening to the fullness of who you are or your multidimensional nature.

To practice this, you should breathe fast and evenly. As you breathe this way, you will alter your state of consciousness, and from this position, you will gain insights into who you are. Think of this as meditation on steroids. One of the tenets of HB holds that you have an inner radar that can point out to you what experiences matter the most at any point in time. Still, you can't have conscious awareness of what this experience might be until you have it.

How could this help you with astral projection? Use this before you go to bed or before projecting. You'll have all the energy you need to generate and maintain your astral body and keep up the stability you need to move around the astral plane without getting lost. Breathing this way helps increase dimethyltryptamine or DMT in your body. The rapid, even breath causes oxygenated blood to flood your brain and encourages its production in your pineal gland. This means your dreams and projections will be crisp and clear.

How to Breathe Holotropically

For your first experience, it helps to have a partner as a spotter while you do this, so you feel at ease with wherever your mind goes. Do not try this if you suffer from low or high blood pressure, cardiovascular diseases, or glaucoma. Also, be aware that strong emotions tend to arise due to this breath-work, sometimes in conjunction with suppressed, painful memories.

1. Make sure your room is cool and dark.

2. Lie down on your back on the floor, and make sure you're comfortable. You can use a mat if you want to.

3. Put on an eye mask, so you don't see any light, or you can just shut your eyes.

4. Allow all tension to melt away from your body as you take some relaxing breaths to release the tension in your muscles.

5. When you sense you're ready, breathe deeper, inhaling through your nose and allowing your belly to rise as far as it can.

6. Feel your stomach deflate as you exhale.

7. Pick up the pace with your breath while making sure your mind remains free and clear. To help maintain a clear mind, you may repeat mentally or under your breath, "Inhale, exhale." Keep this up until you sense you're in an altered state of consciousness.

Why Breathing Matters in Astral Projection

Relax better. When you breathe the right way, you relax a lot more. Being relaxed is essential because it's how you get the vibrations that allow your astral body to step out of the physical one. Breathing deep, slow, and rhythmically allows your mind to slow down, brings your blood pressure to a balanced point, and helps your chakras open up. Every cell in your body benefits from your deep breathing, and you're more in tune with the subtler energies you will be merging with shortly.

At the start, your breathing is deep. Then, the more your body relaxes, the shorter the rhythm of your breath will be, and eventually, it's almost like you're not even breathing at all. This is the stage of peak relaxation.

Slow your brain activity to access your subconscious mind. In other words, when you breathe in a calm, relaxed rhythm, you slow down your brainwave activity. Typically, in waking consciousness, our brainwaves are in the frequencies of Gamma and Beta, which are very active. When you meditate or breathe slow, the activity drops to Alpha, Theta, or even as deep as Delta. These frequencies are the best for creative thought and astral projection.

As you go deeper, your body goes to sleep while your mind opens up the subconscious for you to work with as you please. The subconscious is essential when it comes to astral projecting. This is the point where you experience hypnagogia. You see colorful patterns and sometimes snatches of images just before entering the vibrational state to separate from your body.

Boost your concentration and focus. Whatever breathing technique you use requires you to focus on your breath as you follow its flow from nostrils to the belly and back. This makes it hard for your monkey mind to hop around as it likes to, and as a result, you can deepen your relaxation. This means when you're in the astral realm, you can simply use your breath to remain calm and focused on the tasks you set out to accomplish there.

Stimulate your chakras. Your chakras must be activated before you leave your body, or you might have a hard time working with your astral body. Breath-work allows you to activate and clean out these energy centers. All you have to do is pay attention to each one in turn as you breathe. You can visualize life force or a beautiful bluish light moving into each chakra as you inhale and then see the chakra glow brighter as you exhale. For reference, you have seven major chakras:

- The root chakra, at the base of your spine or the perineum.

- The sacral chakra, just below your belly button.

- The solar plexus chakra, right in between and beneath your ribs.

- The heart chakra, in the center of your chest.

- The throat chakra, in the middle of your neck.

- The third eye chakra, in between and just above your eyebrows.

- The crown chakra, in the center of your head, on top.

Breathing Exercises

Let's get into some breathing exercises that you can do independently without a guide or a pricey facilitator. If you want to do them with a friend, you can do that. Do note some people react intensely to these exercises. So, if it starts to feel a bit much for you, please take a break and try another day.

Alternate Nostril Breathing

This is also called *Nadi Shodhana*, which is a subtle energy clearing method of breathing. It's an ancient yoga breathing method that helps you find inner peace and release anxiety and stress. It also helps to ground you and gets rid of insomnia. Your focus will sharpen. Both hemispheres of your brain will balance out and work in harmony, and you'll also clear out all the blocked chakras in your body. In addition to all of this, toxins will be eliminated from your body,

1. Sit somewhere quiet and comfortable, in the lotus pose if you prefer.

2. Place your left hand on your left knee.

3. Put your right hand up to your nose.

4. Exhale, emptying your lungs.

5. Using your right thumb, press down on your right nostril.

6. Breathe in through your left one, then press down on it with your fingers.

7. Take your thumb off the right nostril and exhale through it.

8. Inhale with your right nostril, and then exhale with the left. That's a complete cycle.

9. Repeat this for five minutes. Make sure to finish by exhaling with the left nostril.

The 4-7-8 Method

Don't have enough time? Then this method is just for you. You can use it to connect with your emotions and body and give your nervous system a much-needed break while you're at it.

1. Find a quiet, comfy place to sit.

2. Shut your eyes, and inhale through your nose for four seconds.

3. Hold your breath for seven seconds.

4. Finally, exhale through your slightly parted lips for 8 seconds, using force so that you hear a "whooshing" sound.

5. Do this cycle four times in a session.

Soft Belly Breathing

In a perfect world, we'd all be breathing from our abdomen. However, we don't. So, this is an excellent exercise to do each day. It helps you deal with nervous tension, anxious thoughts, and stress so that you can find that peaceful center within you. The key is to keep the belly soft and breathe without force. If you force it, you will feel even more anxious and wonder why it isn't working.

1. Sit on a chair or on the floor, making sure you're comfortable.

2. Shut your eyes, and take a few deep relaxing breaths, in through your nose and out through your slightly parted lips.

3. Allow your body to become very rooted to the chair or floor. Again, there's no force here, just a pleasant heaviness.

4. As you inhale, let the air move into your belly. Keep your stomach soft.

5. Exhale with no effort. The belly should remain soft.

6. It may help if you mentally repeat the words "soft" as you breathe in and "belly" as you exhale and release all tension and resistance.

7. With each breath you take in, visualize it taking care of your belly. With each exhale, allow your breath to flood you with warm relaxation, diffusing all tension in you, in thoughts, body, and emotions.

8. As emotion is held in the belly, the process of breathing softly like this will cause memories, images, and thoughts to come up. Whatever you get, welcome it all. If you notice you're engaging with these thoughts and emotions, be glad you did, and gently return your mind to your breathing.

9. Once five to ten minutes have passed, put your hands on your stomach. Notice the breath as it pushes your belly softly into your hands.

10. Bit by bit, begin to allow your awareness to flow into the space all around you.

11. End this session with an intention to remain connected to your belly and your breath as you gently come out of the meditative state.

Circular Breathing

You must do this mindfully and as gently as possible because this breathing technique can alter your consciousness. The goal is to breathe in and out with no breaks in between. You can do this quietly or make a whooshing sound on every exhale. Expect that old emotions might come up. This means you are releasing old, stale energy in your emotional body and allowing your mind to open up to deeper levels of truth.

1. Sit in a comfy position.

2. Inhale and exhale through your nose.

3. Count each inhalation and exhalation, making sure they're the same number of seconds.

4. If you like, you can include a slight pause to retain your breath between inhales and exhales. Only do this if it feels comfortable.

5. Keep this up for at least five minutes.

Visualization Breathing

There are a lot of ways you can visualize as you breathe deeply. Your visualization should fit whatever your present needs are. Here are your options:

1. See your energy centers glowing as you breathe prana or life force into them.

2.   See divine light moving through your body as you breathe in and out, washing all over you.

3.   See the pathway air takes as it moves through your respiratory system.

4.   See tension and stress melting off your body as you breathe out.

5.   Breathe in light into your chakras and breathe out darkness.

6.   Inhale pain, and exhale loving-kindness (This is Ton-glen, a Buddhist practice).

Remember, your breath is life itself. Practice these exercises to make sure that you give your astral body the energy it needs to move around the astral plane.

Chapter Eight: Self-Hypnosis

You're driving home from work, and you suddenly realize you're pulling into your driveway. You don't quite remember the details of the trip. Still, you've driven this route enough times that it's become second nature. So, your mind focused on other thoughts, leaving just enough consciousness for you to be aware of what you were doing and spot any potential danger along the way.

You're reading a hard-to-put-down novel, and things are really escalating with the protagonist. Your heart is racing. It feels like you're in there, in the thick of things, and not holding a book in your hands reading along. It's noisy all around you, but you don't care. All you hear and see are the voices of the characters and the world around *them*.

Self-Hypnosis Defined

What's going on in each of these instances? Self-hypnosis. This is a trance state that we slip into on a day-to-day basis. It's a natural phenomenon that happens when you have laser focus, keeping your attention trained on just one thing. It also happens when you're doing something routine, like when you brush your teeth or shower. That's why you have the most brilliant ideas while you're in the shower, by the way. Your conscious mind goes on autopilot, which allows the solutions to whatever challenges you're facing to float into your conscious awareness from the subconscious mind.

Being in a state of hypnosis allows your mind to become very open to suggestions. This is something you can take advantage of, as you can suggest things to yourself that you'd love to experience. For example, you can suggest to yourself that you will astral project tonight and that you'll find it pleasant and enjoyable. You can also tell yourself that you'll make a stop at your Aunt Edna's on your trip to see how she's doing.

Hypnosis is a state of hyper-focus. You become absorbed with the moment, or the task at hand, or whatever it is you've chosen to place your attention on. You don't have to work with a therapist to induce this state. Instead, you can put yourself in it, following the proper technique. Once you master this, it's like having a skeleton key that unlocks all the doors to everything you want in life. You'll be the master of your thoughts, in charge of your reactions and emotions.

One of the most fantastic things about hypnotizing yourself is that you can do this anywhere, anytime. It also helps that you're the one in charge, so you don't have to worry about a hypnotist giving your subconscious mind suggestions that you don't totally agree with. Instead, you get to decide what the suggestions should be, and you save yourself a ton of money by choosing to be your own therapist.

The Role of Self-Hypnosis in Astral Projection

With the right state of mind, you can accomplish anything. Never underestimate the value of focus. Having a focused mind equals having a powerful life. You'll find it easier to perform amazing feats in your career, no matter what field you're in. You'll be better at dealing with all kinds of pain, and your creativity goes through the roof as well.

With the hyper-focus of self-hypnosis, you can gain a lot more confidence when facing the unknown. The astral is a realm that constantly surprises travelers with strange, new things. Some of these things may delight you, and others may worry you if you don't get yourself together and face those situations with a healthy mix of courage and curiosity. When you're frightened in the astral, you attract more to be afraid of. You'll also find it harder to project because you don't want to experience those scary things again. Self-hypnosis can help you shed the fear and take a bold leap into the unknown.

Trying to make things happen using just the conscious mind can sometimes be a bit of an uphill climb. When it comes to changing a habit or setting yourself free from fears, it helps to work with the subconscious. This is where the belief patterns that cause those undesirable situations emerge from, making change a tedious, slow process. When you hypnotize yourself, you take your brainwaves down to Theta. In this state, you're less inhibited and very open to new ideas and thought patterns. From this state, you can mold yourself into the person you'd rather be.

The astral is an alternate state of consciousness, one which you can get into using hypnosis. With it, you can will yourself through its various levels to learn more and become a fully evolved soul.

If you find it difficult to remember your projections, self-hypnosis can rescue you. You don't recall them because your astral consciousness didn't make that connection to your physical brain for you to download them. This could happen because you've never put much stock in such things as astral travel, to begin with. Suggesting to yourself in a state of hypnosis that you always remember your trips will help you connect the physical you and astral you.

Self-Hypnosis versus Meditation

These practices are almost the same thing. Of course, you need to be in a calm, relaxed state of mind to make any headway with either. However, with self-hypnosis, you have a specific goal that you'd like to achieve so that you can live a better quality of life.

In meditation, you don't have a goal. You simply sit and allow whatever floats into your mind to do so, without labeling or controlling it, without any intention on your part. Both practices will give you a remarkable boost in your mental and physical health, giving to you in so many ways. It is worthwhile to devote equal time to both practices.

Getting into a Trance for Astral Projection

Here's a step-by-step method for getting into a deep trance state.

1. Lie down, shut your eyes, and breathe with the intent to feel relaxed and calm.

2. When you feel a pleasant wave of relaxation flow through your body, imagine you're going down a ladder in the dark. Don't see the ladder in your mind's eye. Just feel your hands and feet on the rungs as you descend.

3. On each exhale, feel your body climbing down the ladder. A step or two should do.

4. On each inhale, simply feel your hands and feet on the ladder.

5. As you go down, stir up a sensation of falling within your mind. This will change your brainwave level from Beta (alert and awake) to Alpha (asleep) and then to Theta (deeper sleep). You're in a trance once you hit the Alpha level.

6. Continue with this exercise for as long as you need. The more experience you have with deep relaxation and stilling your mind, the faster you will enter the trance state.

7. When you notice a feeling of heaviness wash over you, you can stop the falling sensation in your mind. Also, suppose you don't like the idea of a ladder. In that case, you can simply imagine you're in an elevator and simulate that falling sensation on each exhale.

What You Should Know About Getting into a Deep Trance

The depth of your trance is determined by your ability to concentrate, relax, and use your willpower. If you want to get into deeper levels from Theta and beyond, you'll need to keep your focus on the breath and falling sensation for much longer. That being said, the first trance level is more than enough for you to have a projection. You'll know you've achieved this trance level when you feel pretty heavy.

Make sure before you attempt to get into a deep trance you've had some experience with light trance. You'll know you're getting into a deep trance when:

- You feel uncomfortably cold. You're not shivering, just losing body heat.

- In your mind, you feel very weird.

- Everything feels too, too slow.

- Your thoughts have slowed down to the point where it feels like you've been drugged.

- You feel very removed from your body, as if you're floating, and everything is too far from you.

- You are completely paralyzed, unable to move.

When these signs happen *simultaneously*, then you're bordering on a deep trance. The feeling of floating is a lot milder with a light trance as your astral body begins to separate from the physical one. The same can be said for the loss of body heat and paralysis. Those happen in a light trance, but it's to a lesser degree and not as uncomfortable as a deep trance.

You don't have to worry about accidentally triggering a deep trance state, though. This can only happen when you've put in a lot of work to relax fully while staying alert. It also takes a lot of mental energy and willpower. Keep in mind that you can snap out of a trance anytime you wish, and this should mitigate whatever fears you might have. To come out of a trance, simply focus all your willpower on moving your fingers or toes. When you're able to move something, even if it's just a pinky, use that momentum to move the rest of your body. Then, get up and get out of bed. Move around a bit for some minutes. Otherwise, if you go right back to lie down, you might slip back in again.

What to Expect in a Trance

When you're in a trance, you will feel mildly paralyzed. But, right along with this, you'll notice subtle energy that seems to encompass your body. This energy might feel like a gentle tickle all over your body. Then, it will build in intensity, becoming the vibrations every projector knows. It's a feeling of buzzing with electricity all over your body, and it can be pleasant if you don't react with fear or try to fight it.

This vibration happens as your astral body expands to allow more energy in. It will use this energy to move around in the astral plane. This happens every time you go to sleep, except now, you're observing it consciously. As you vibrate, your astral body will begin to drift from your physical one, slightly out of sync with it.

Another Self-Hypnosis Method

1. Find somewhere comfortable for you to relax. If you're sitting, use a soft chair, and keep your feet and legs uncrossed. You can lie down if you prefer, but you should try sitting instead if you find that you just fall asleep each time.

2. Make sure you're wearing loose clothing for this.

3. Don't eat heavily before you attempt this.

4. Make sure there will be no distractions or interruptions for the next twenty to thirty minutes.

5. Breathe deeply, in through your nose, and out through your slightly parted lips. You want your abdomen to rise and fall with each breath so that your body gets all the oxygen it needs to foster your transition to an altered state of consciousness, thanks to DMT.

6. Now, use progressive muscle relaxation. To do this, scan your body from the soles of your feet to the crown of your head. You're looking for any tension. When you notice tension, let it melt away as you exhale. You can also tense the muscles for a second and then release them as you exhale, allowing yourself to fall deeper into relaxation.

7. As you release the tension, you can imagine it as a dark cloud that floats out of those tight spots and away, dissipating into nothing.

8. As you breathe in, imagine that your breath is a bright light, the very essence of life itself. See that light coursing through your body, removing all tension and resistance, bringing you to a state of total relaxation. Allow the light to leave you pleasantly warm. See it as a blanket that pleasantly envelopes you, keeping you safe, opening up your mind to receive the seeds you wish to plant in it.

9. Now it's time to make your suggestions. You're in a state of focused relaxation, and you can now plant the ideas you want your subconscious to work with to make you better at astral projecting. Make simple statements in the present tense and with positive wording. Keep your attitude open and trusting.

10. Next, come back to your regular waking consciousness. Don't be in a hurry, though. Count to five, as you suggest to yourself that you'll become aware of your environment. When you hit the count of five, slowly open your eyes, acknowledge that you've been transformed with gratitude, and then go about your day.

Tips for Using Suggestions

Use conviction. Don't just think or say the words without feeling their meaning. Instead, say them with confidence and a positive attitude.

Again, always use present tense. Using present continuous tense keeps your goal perpetually in the future, ever unreachable. Remember, "I *am*," not "I *will be.*"

Keep it positive. "I am a successful astral projector," not "I am not a failure at astral projection." Focus on what you prefer, not the stuff you'd rather not experience.

Keep it realistic. Don't get too ambitious by saying, "I will go to the highest planes of the astral realm in just two days." Keep your goals small and specific, and you're more likely to attain them. As you smash these goals, you'll grow in confidence, and then with time, you'll be ready for the bigger stuff. Simply choosing to see the Eiffel tower, or visit a loved one, or fly over your neighborhood isn't a bad place to start.

Repeat, repeat, repeat. The more you repeat these suggestions during your trance state, the deeper they will take root, and the more successful you'll be in achieving your goals.

The Power of Trance

Entering the trance state to make suggestions to yourself can lead to transformations that will leave your jaw hanging to the floor. I cannot begin to tell you all the ways I've personally used self-hypnosis to take my life from terrible to a literal fairytale.

Am I insinuating that you can rid yourself of all the problems you have in one fell swoop? No. What I am saying is that self-hypnosis is a highly underrated tool to help you master the game of life. You can use this as a tool to create behavioral changes in yourself that will then lead you to the solutions or improved circumstances you seek.

And if that doesn't float your boat, well, you could simply focus on using this to shorten the learning curve of astral projection.

Here's a neat thing to do when you make it out of your body. Ask for your guide to show up, trusting that they will. First, express your gratitude to your guide for coming. Then, ask them to tell you anything you need to know to help you get better at astral projection. They will give you bespoke information based on your specific needs, which will beat anything you could read in any book—including mine. Who knows, they just might tell you, "All you need to do is blink three times in a trance state, and you're out in the astral realm!" Now wouldn't *that* be cool!

Chapter Nine: Affirming Your Goals

Affirmations are short sentences that you state with firm conviction to achieve your goals and dreams and reach the highest heights of your potential. You repeat them often so that you can imprint them on your subconscious. Your subconscious can, in turn, take those sentences to help you change your pattern of thoughts, beliefs, habits, and paradigms so that they all line up with what you affirm.

When you "affirm" something, you declare it to be true, which automatically implies that you phrase your affirmations as very real facts grounded in the present.

Why Affirmations Work

Pick up any book on affirmations or hop on any blog post or random YouTube video, and they'll tell you that there's power in words. Well, you're not going to get that here.

Affirmations work not because there's power in the words you choose, but because of the meaning and intention you put into them. If words were powerful, we'd all be doomed. It just doesn't work like that.

So, you may wonder, how do affirmations achieve such powerful effects? How do they make things happen? The answer is, they don't—*you* do. The affirmation process is simply the conscious, focused use of your mind to craft a life that you'd prefer. That's it.

Recall that the power lies within you, and it only really shines through when you make friends with the principle of focus. The more focus you bring to the here and now, the better your results will be. So, affirmations are a focusing tool that allow you to change your world, reflecting your preferences.

Using Affirmations for Astral Projecting

Now, we're going to put together two excellent practices to give you incredible results with astral projection. First, we're going to combine astral projection with hypnosis. Done right, you should have no problems with leaving your body.

Hypnosis gives you direct access to your pleasure centers and sensory-motor cortex. You also work with your lower cerebral portions (which handle emotions) and the pleasure centers in the right hemisphere of your brain. This process naturally happens when you disengage the left brain's self-cognitive function, so it no longer screens stimulus as it should. So, when you hypnotize yourself, you can plant ideas in your head that will take root and give you your desired outcome.

Your left brain classifies all incoming information, assessing all the data streaming through your senses and giving them meaning before letting them through to the right brain. On the other hand, your right brain is noncritical. It handles information holistically and finds patterns in occurrences and all stimuli you get. It accepts what the left brain feeds it with zero questions asked. So, when you distract the left brain with boredom or put it in a trance state, it's easy for affirmations to reach your right brain. Untainted by the left brain's interpretations, the affirmations can work their magic. For example, suppose your goal is to astral project for the first time or get better at leaving your body. In that case, you will find the best results by administering suggestions to your right brain or subconscious from a trance state that you are a pro at this.

Affirmations for Astral Projection

The following are affirmations you can use to supercharge your ability to leave your body. You may reword them to feel more natural to you or use them as they are. Either way, you need to make sure you really feel the meaning of the words and uncritically accept them as accurate.

- I am more than just my physical body.

- I am consciousness in its purest form.

- I perceive things that are beyond the physical realm with ease.

- I have access to higher realms of existence.

- I am exploring these realms, one way or another, learning more about my multi-dimensional self.

- I freely receive the help and wisdom of all beings whose level of understanding of the astral realm is greater than mine.

- I freely receive guidance along my travels.

- I freely receive protection from benevolent beings with my best interests at heart.

- I am always loved and protected by my guides.

- I am light; therefore, I only attract that which is light.

- I am good; therefore, I only attract good beings and entities of high vibration.

- I am full of positive intentions; therefore, I only interact with positive beings and experiences.

- I am in control of my emotions.

- I am calm during my projections, maintaining my focus with ease.

- I am a master of leaving the physical realm to explore the astral.

- I find it so easy to leave my body.

- I find it easy to maintain my consciousness in the astral.

- I have impeccable recall and remember every detail of my astral travels.

- Regardless of how my day goes, I astral project each night.

- I am love, loving, and loved.

- I am love, and love drives out all fear.

Besides these affirmations to help you out with your astral trip, you should consider setting intentions to help you achieve very definite objectives.

Setting Intentions for Astral Projection

When you finally make it out of your body, you'll find your journey more rewarding when you know what you want to achieve before you even leave your body.

In other words, before you project, you set an intention. For example, you may decide that you'd like to speak with your guides and ask them what you need to know the most at this stage of your life to advance further. Or your goal may be to channel healing energy to a loved one who could use it or travel to a particular time and place in the past, future, or alternate present. You may intend to hear a piece of music to help you in your composition or get an idea for a movie script or vaccine. As you can probably tell, there are no limits to the intentions you can set.

What if you don't want to intend anything? Couldn't you roam freely in the astral? Well, you can, but chances are you'll find your consciousness fizzling out if you don't give it something to focus on via your intention. On the other hand, if you think you'd rather see where things take you, then you should firmly set that as an intention while in the trance state or shortly before you go (back) to bed. Still, it's best to plan whatever it is you want to accomplish in advance so that you don't wind up roaming the astral plane and forgetting you're projecting.

For instance, after working on a book for several hours and hitting a bit of a block about what else to add to it, I decided I'd call it a night and head to bed. That night, I astral projected and found myself in a library. It was the most extensive, grandest library I'd *ever* seen, physically speaking, of course. But, unfortunately, I hadn't planned to project, so I had no intentions in mind. As a result, I found myself wandering away from the library and being distracted by other stuff going on. It wasn't until I woke up that I realized, had I set a clear intention, I could have perhaps opened up some of those books with the intent to get fresh ideas for mine!

Without a clear intention, it's not unusual to immediately head from a projection to a regular dream. Sure, the dream will most definitely have a more vibrant, "real" quality to it, but then, you lose out on the chance to be a conscious traveler. So as soon as you're out of your body, get as far away from your body as possible. It's better if it's out of sight. After that, you can turn your attention back to your intention right away.

How to Set Intentions

The very process of thinking about what you're going to do when you project just before you do is often more than enough. However, you can make this intention even more solid by stating it in a trance state.

Let's assume you'd like to check out the other side of the moon tonight. You would need to get into outer space, somehow. You could decide you're going to get there with a rocket launcher, a spaceship, a flying car, or by simply flying over there. You might decide you want to create a portal for you to walk through, which will take you right to the moon's other side. You could also intend for there to be light over the entire area, so you don't find yourself in the dark or with poor astral sight, unable to see anything.

Setting your chosen intention involves repeating a simple statement in your mind that summarizes what you're going to do. Then, to further cement your intention, you can mentally rehearse all the actions you're going to take in your head. Mental rehearsals help, too. When you finally carry out your plan in the astral, you'll have done it enough times to get rid of the emotion of excitement. It's understandable why you'd feel that rush, but it can distract you or take you out of the moment.

Understand you don't have to set intentions to take care of every little detail. That would leave little room for surprise or other elements that might help you discover new ways to grow. It's like opening the map app on your phone and knowing how to get from Ohio to California. Sure, you can see the route, but you have no idea who you'll run into or what you'll experience along the way.

There's no clock on this. Don't feel like you need to hurry to see your intention through to the end. I feel the need to stress this, so you don't get mad at yourself if you keep projecting and yet haven't followed through on your intention. If it helps, you may move on to another plan. If your plan to create a portal isn't working, understand you can get where you're going through other means. It helps to have backup intentions so that your astral travel is still worth your while.

For instance, you could have a backup intention of increasing your presence and awareness to the point where everything is stable in the astral. You can see, hear, touch, taste, and smell things and focus on making them feel so real you'd be questioning whether or not you projected. Another thing to do is have conversations with the beings or entities you encounter. See what they have to say and pay attention. This way, you can gain insight into your life and some inspiration as well.

You'll find that the most rewarding astral trips are those where you set out to make something happen before you leave your body, and you actually do. Setting your intention gives you a huge advantage. You can predict that you'll run into irrational stuff, which will prepare you for any challenge you face. This foresight is a good thing, especially if you find yourself struggling to remain stable and focused in the astral—a common problem when you're just starting. So set your intentions while you're awake, and you'll do just great.

5 Ways to Set Powerful Intentions

Find the gap between your thoughts. The mind is a busy place, constantly processing emotions, thoughts, and memories like the time you stepped out of the restroom, not knowing your fly was down, and so on. However, there are pauses in between all of these activities. Sometimes the break is so short, so fleeting that you don't notice it. The way to start noticing the space between your thoughts is to make a habit of meditating. As you meditate, you surpass the ego-mind and become pure consciousness or the silence or gap between thoughts. One of the best times to set your intentions for powerful results is in this gap.

Let your desires and intentions go. When you have set your intentions, the next thing to do is to let them go. Letting them go implies that you implicitly trust that they are a done deal, and you will see their manifestation in due time. So, you want to be deliberate about letting go. It's the attitude you have when you've ordered a pizza. You don't keep checking at the window to see if it's going to get here, and you don't keep calling the pizza place to hound them about whether or not they're going to get it to you. You know it's yours, so you're relaxed and at ease.

Remain grounded in a state of divine nonchalance. If you want to turbocharge your intentions, then you want to set them from a place of power. You can't fix them when you're feeling desperate or needy or you believe you lack something. So always set them from a place of contentment and ease. Other people's opinions and your present circumstances should not affect the fact that you know your intentions are set and done. You have no idea how or when your plan will play out, but you know it's a done deal, and your higher self is on the case.

Detach yourself from the outcome. Some people worry that if they practice detachment, they will not get the results that they want. Don't bind yourself to a particular scenario. If you want security, then you must embrace uncertainty. This seems like a paradox, but that's how life works. True security lies in abandoning yourself to All That Is, trusting it knows the perfect way to give you what you need when you need it. When you are attached to getting a specific outcome, it just means you're full of fear and feeling very insecure. Detachment is a statement of one hundred percent trust in the power that lies in your true self. Make your intentions, acknowledge that they are working out as they should, and then let go. Things will then unfold in a way to bring you to your desired end. Detachment isn't giving up. It's allowing things to play out in your favor. Don't interfere with the process.

Delegate to the universe. When you have a focused intention, you rally all the forces of the intelligent universe, Source, or All That Is, to get moving on your behalf. Your job is to trust that the very force that causes the sun to rise, keeps the planets in alignment, and grows the grass is the same one taking care of you. The difference is, where nature allows this force to do what it must, man tends to get in the way with fear, doubt, and worry. So, assign the fulfillment of your intention to the universe. Don't give in to the need to obsess or become overly vigilant. That does you no good. If you try to force a result, you won't like what comes of it. Instead, allow it to play out naturally by planting your intentions in a field fertile with pure potential. They will bloom and grow when the time is right.

Part Three: Getting in the Astral Plane

Chapter Ten: Preparing to Project

You don't just decide to run a marathon without adequate preparation. The same thing applies to learning to leave your physical body. So, in this chapter, we're going to cover everything you need to be ready for before your first projection.

Best Time to Astral Travel

There's no right or wrong time to project. It all comes down to what works for you in the end. Some people find that projecting right before bedtime is ideal. Others say it's better to leave in the early hours of the morning after you've slept for a bit so that you're still in that sleepy, drowsy state. However, you can leave your body anytime you want to.

If you fear the dark, then it might be best to practice astral projection during the day. This is ideal because your fear of the dark won't have a chance to play out in the astral realm as an unpleasant experience. You're far less likely to manifest or attract malevolent beings or thought-forms. You must deal with this fear before you practice at night. The last thing you want is to be put off astral projection forever because of one frightful experience.

There are more reasons you should project in the morning after you've had some sleep, besides having the benefit of light, especially if you're just starting. For one thing, trying to project when you're exhausted at the end of the day might cause you to be less disciplined about the procedure. In addition, you'll probably be too tired to keep your mind awake as your body shuts down for the night. Also, you may struggle to ignore the impulse to scratch an itch or rollover when you should be perfectly still.

So, it's better to project after you've had some sleep—not enough to make you wide awake and alert, but just enough to give you some energy. Say you get eight hours of sleep at night (or per day, if you work nights or something). The best time to wake up would be about three to four hours in. You need the mini recharge from those hours. Still, it also helps to be in a drowsy state with your body already relaxed, so you can slip out easier than if you tried to do it right from a wakeful state.

Setting Up Your Space

You can't afford distractions. So, eliminate as much sound and light as possible. Turn off your phone. Make sure there are no alarms that could turn it back on and pull you out of your mind-awake, body-asleep state. If you would rather leave your phone on because that's where you document your travels and dreams, then make sure that all alerts and alarms are set to silent.

Earplugs are good to have. The last thing you want is to finally reach the vibration phase of projection, only to come out of it because the neighbor decided that was a good time to play some head-banging music. Also, a sleep mask will help you a lot if light makes it hard for you to go back to bed. Keep the curtains drawn as well, if that helps.

If you share a bed with someone, you might find it very distracting when they roll over or get out of bed. Rather than get mad, consider swapping out your shared bed for twin beds, which you can keep close together but without touching. This way, your partner can roll over, get out of bed, and you won't be bothered one bit. If twin beds aren't an option, think about getting a mat. You don't have to sleep on it all night. You only move to it when you're projecting. The only other solution would be for you to move to a couch. Just make sure you're as comfortable as you can be, so you don't have to return prematurely from your trip because of a crick in your neck or something.

Sleeping Positions

You'll increase the odds of success if you lie down in a position that's unusual for you. For example, if you tend to sleep on your side or your stomach, try sleeping on your back instead so you can slow down the process of falling asleep enough to control it.

One thing you will find helpful is to start in a semi-upright position. If you have a recliner, then that's great. Otherwise, you can prop yourself up on pillows so that you're almost sitting up, but not quite. This doesn't mean you can't practice while lying down, but if you find that you often slip off into sleep before you can project, then it just might help to elevate the top half of your body somehow.

Resisting Impulses

You've spent your whole life going to bed by allowing your mind to sleep right along with your body. Judging by the fact that you're reading this, you've definitely built this habit up over years and years, which means it's going to be a particularly tricky one to break. Astral projection requires that you keep your mind awake while your body enters a state of sleep. So, let's go over what you need to do to develop the appropriate sleep habits, starting with resisting impulses.

To successfully project, you need to get to a mind-awake-body-asleep state. Typically, when you're about to drift off to sleep, your body will test your mind to see if it's awake. It will make your itch so bad you want to scratch it, or you'll feel the need to roll over, turn, or adjust your body. The only reason to give in to the latter impulse is if you weren't in a comfortable position to begin with, so you should address this before you start the process. As for the itches, there's nothing to do but resist them.

Sometimes they will hit you in multiple spots at once. They can be very persistent. Just don't scratch. If you simply observe them as a detached third party or keep your mind occupied with other things, it will pass after about ten to fifteen seconds. Interestingly, the second you raise your hand to scratch yourself, the itch disappears. It's like your body says, "Gotcha! I knew you were awake." So, don't give in to the urge.

Another thing you want to avoid is swallowing. If you swallow, it could slow down the process or cause you to have to start from scratch. To help you avoid this, elevate your head with pillows so that the urge is minimized.

Your eyes also tend to move around a lot. But, again, this is a habit from ordinary waking consciousness. When you shut your eyes, you may notice this movement. It may seem trivial, but this makes it hard for beginners to shut their bodies down. Turn both eyes towards the third eye, which is in the center of your forehead, just above the brows. Your eyes should be shut while doing this, of course. When you focus them on the third eye, it stops them from twitching, trying to see what's going on. Your body will fall asleep faster when you hold your eyes still this way.

The Thin Line between Sleep and Wakefulness

The successful astral projector knows how vital it is to maintain conscious awareness in the state between sleep and wakefulness. To execute this feat flawlessly, you need to keep your conscious mind busy with something. Whatever you do, don't keep it focused on thoughts that are too exciting, or on your problems, or what you're supposed to do tomorrow because that's a recipe for insomnia.

The best thing to do is have a mantra that you repeat over and over. It could be as simple as "Mind awake, body asleep." You repeat this in your mind, not out loud. For some people, it's hard to keep repeating a mantra because that lulls them to sleep. So, the better option is to count down from three-hundred to one. The great thing about this countdown is that it's a monotonous task, but it also keeps your mind active enough so that it doesn't fall asleep on you.

Now sometimes, you may find you've drifted off as you count. When this happens, and you catch yourself, don't sweat it. Just pick up where you left off counting, or pick any random number and resume counting from there. You don't need to be accurate. You just need to keep your mind up and busy.

Don't beat yourself up if you notice you keep drifting to sleep. This is actually a good thing if you know how to work with it. The more you practice hovering between sleep and wakefulness, the more likely you'll have successful astral trips. Also, the more you dip in and out of sleep, the closer you will get to the vibration phase (which starts with feeling a pleasant heaviness rolling up from your feet to your head).

To get better at pulling your mind out of sleep, you can use the method suggested by Robert Monroe. Lie on your back and keep one forearm up in the air. When you slip into sleep, it will drop, causing you to wake up again. If you find this uncomfortable, you can attach a weight to a piece of string and then tie the other end of the rope around a finger. Next, allow your hand to hang over the bed, holding the weight in it. When you slip into sleep, your hand will release the weight, and the force of it dropping will yank your finger, which will jolt your mind back awake. The more you practice this, the sooner you'll be able to maintain this in-between state without needing any props or unique positions to help you out.

Yoga Poses for Astral Projection

Before you astral project, you can take advantage of yoga to help you increase the odds in your favor. Ideally, these moves should be routine for you, and you should do them in a fluid movement, moving from one pose to the next. They'll help you remain alert yet relaxed, which is excellent for astral travel. You'll be more likely to stay up. The poses are easy to master, so don't worry about needing to be an acrobat or a contortionist.

Urdhva Hastasana (Upward Hand Pose): Stand with both feet hip's width apart. Move your arms right out in front of you from your side. Lift them fully over your head and stretch upwards, with your palms facing each other. Allow this stretch to work your sides, shoulders, back, and stomach. Release this pose by allowing your hands to come back down, the same way you lifted them.

Upward Hand Pose

Uttanasana (Forward Bend): You bend over at the hips as you exhale from the previous pose. Bring your chest to your knees. Keep them as close as possible without forcing them, placing your hands on the floor beside your feet or on just below your knees. Again, don't force the stretch. You'll feel this stretch in the calves, hamstrings, and lower back.

Forward Bend

Bhujangasana (Cobra Pose): From the forward bend, walk out on your hands, ensuring your body weight is evenly distributed between your hands and feet. Walk until you're in a full plank position, and then gently allow your lower abs and legs to rest on the floor. The tops of your feet should be flat on the ground if you can manage that. To make things easier, if you can't handle a plank, just lie on your stomach, keeping your arms flat and beside your belly. Then, with your elbows bent, raise your head and chest. You'll notice your shoulder blades squeezing in the middle while your chest muscles open up.

Cobra Pose

Adho Mukha Svanasana (Downward-Facing Dog): From the cobra pose, just go back into the plank position and pull your hips back. Your hands, still flat on the floor, should be extended in front of you. Done right, your body will resemble an upside-down "V." Relax into this stretch, but don't force it.

Downward Facing Dog

Virabhadrasana I (Warrior 1): From downward-facing-dog, bring one foot in between both hands, and then lift your torso. You should have one leg stretched out behind you and the other in front of you, bent. Think of it like a lunge, except your back foot lines up with the front one and also points outwards, slightly. The heel of your front foot should ideally align with the arch of the foot in the back.

Lean into this stretch, and then raise your hands so they're above you. Clasp your hands together. You'll feel this one in your legs, waist, and hips. To get out of this position, move the back leg to meet the front one.

Repeat these moves, ending with Warrior 1 on the opposite legs. You only need a few minutes to finish this routine, but you can repeat it as often as you like. It's a great way to get rid of the tension, which can keep your astral body stuck in the physical if not dealt with.

Warrior 1 Pose

More Helpful Tips for Astral Projection

Practice in the morning. At least in the beginning. Then, as you gain experience, you will be able to travel wherever you want to.

Know your plan beforehand. Are you going to visit a place, a loved one, or a guide? Or do you intend to meditate on health or wealth in the astral plane? Then when you're out, you should know precisely how you're going to do it and have backup plans as well so that each trip is fruitful.

Protect yourself. Ideally, knowing you're safe is more than enough protection. However, if you feel like you need it, you can envision yourself surrounded by golden light or white light. Think of this light like an impenetrable bubble around you, which keeps you safe from all malevolence.

Develop your energy body. You should learn about chakras and how to meditate to keep them clean, open, and energized. They feed both your astral and physical body with the energy needed to function optimally. Meditate on each one. Visualize their colors. Watch them glow brighter as they bloom within you.

Get rid of all jewelry before you project. A fascinating thing that happens when you've got jewelry on is that your entire astral body may leave the physical but can't separate at the points you've got jewelry on. So, leave the beautiful astral cuffs behind. You can wear them when you're back.

Use the right technique for you. When you first start, some methods won't work for you. However, it doesn't mean you can't project. Just give each technique several tries until you find one that's easiest.

Don't allow yourself to be afraid. You have to remain in charge of your mind. Keep your cool, and don't let your emotions get the better of you. Remember, the astral world is influenced by thoughts and feelings, so you can't afford to let your mind feed you ideas that don't help you. Fear will take you to lower astral planes with beings that don't mean well for you. Fill your heart with love by affirming that you are love, loving, and loved. Remember, affirming means you mean *every* word. The more you accept yourself as love, the higher the realms you will visit.

Try darkening the room. I have astral projected in full daylight. In fact, my first astral projection was in full sunlight, with all the curtains up. However, if you find the light is a problem, you can darken the room and see if that helps you. *But!* Make sure there's a little bit of light so you can see around you, especially if you have a fear of the dark.

Read other books and consume materials on astral projection. The more you read, the more you learn. There are always lovely nuggets to be found when learning from others.

Be careful what you wish for. The astral plane affects the physical. So, while you're there, be mindful of what you wish for because you're definitely going to get it.

Master your astral body. When you first leave your body, focus on learning how to use it. Don't try to go places without understanding how it works. To do that, you may remain in your room, but pay no attention to your sleeping body on the bed, so you don't get sucked back in.

Master mental commands. If you find that you can't see properly, you could think with authority, "Improve sight, now!" Are you moving around sluggishly? Think, "Increase energy, now!" Want to go to the sun? Say, "To the sun, now!" These words aren't necessary. With time, you'll find that simply having a firm intention about what you want in the moment is enough to fulfill it.

Be precise with your commands. For instance, suppose you intend to travel back in time to Hitler's era. You need to specify whether it's when he was a baby or already doing damage in power.

You can't interact with physical people. This is because the astral and physical realms are of two different vibrations. So, don't expect to be able to interact with people. That said, every now and then, you might be able to make your presence known or felt, especially with those who are very in touch with their psychic, spiritual selves.

There is no danger to fear. If things feel a bit much, you can always come back to the physical.

Expect your guides. They will show up after some time. You'll know they're your real guides through a sense of inner knowing. The feeling will be unmistakable. So, respect them, appreciate them, and obey what they teach you.

You are free, but you must be responsible for that freedom. Don't use your abilities for evil, and don't invade other people's privacy just for your pleasure. If you're going to do that, it must be for a reason that benefits the greater good.

Chapter Eleven: Focusing with Music and Mantras

Music for Astral Projection

You don't need music to astral project, though you can certainly begin with it if it helps you. However, your goal should be to move on from needing music so that you can focus on your astral journey without having it be affected by the mood of the music.

Having said that, you could listen to Baroque music, like Monteverdi, Purcell, Vivaldi and so on. Music from the Baroque period is usually at about 50 to 80 beats per minute. This is the perfect pace that allows you to get into a state of deep concentration, or the Alpha brainwave frequency, conducive to leaving your body.

Hemi-Sync by the Monroe Institute is definitely worth checking out as well. It is specially designed for astral projections. That said, there are a few people that it just doesn't work for, so don't beat yourself up if you don't notice anything.

Using Shamanic Drumming for Astral Projection

We all experienced one thing when we first came into the world: rhythm. Specifically, the feeling of rhythm, not the sound. Your mother's heartbeat was the first thing you could sense, along with her steady breathing. This is where we first learned of rhythm. It's a primal thing.

When you listen to percussive music, any parts of your astral and physical body that don't have energy flowing through them immediately open up and are filled with vitality. This is further enhanced when you're drumming in a group. This also explains why you can't help but move your body to good music, even if you restrict the movement to tapping. Little wonder then that shamanic power can alter our consciousness.

To make this work for you, you need a partner, or even better, a group of friends you trust. You'll also need some drums. The African talking drum is perfect for this.

Traditionally, shamans would cross over to the other side and come back with information to help everyone around them. So feel free to ask your friends for help as you just might have some beneficial information for them. Their job is to help you with the drumming.

Next, you should make sure you're wearing loose clothing. If you would rather, you can be in your birthday suit (if you're on your own or your trusted friends don't mind, of course). The point is you should be comfortable, regardless of the temperature. Also, make sure you don't eat right before trying to project, but that you're not hungry either.

Get rid of all distractions and have your friends surround you in a circle. You're going to chant your mantra as your friends drum. Help them understand that the drumming needs to go from soft and slow to loud and frenzied as they notice you getting exhausted from going around the circle. Of course, if you prefer to work alone, that's fine too. You can find shamanic drumming music on Spotify or Deezer or check YouTube for the most liked ones to use.

Set your intentions. You should know what you're going to do once you're out of your body. Keeping your intentions in mind, you may take a moment to pay your respects to your astral guide and thank them in advance for their help with your journey.

Now it's time to dance around the circle in a clockwise motion. Move in time with the drums, feeling their impact on your heart center. Once you've made about three trips around, you'll notice your state of mind will shift. When you just can't go on, you're at what's called "the runner's wall."

Envision that this wall is the ground, and it's in the middle of the circle. With what's left of your strength, fall on that wall. Allow the momentum of your dance to take you down to the ground. Think of that momentum as astral energy empowering you, and imagine your guide riding that energy wave right along with you. Once you connect with the floor, feel your astral body break right through that wall. Feel your mind bursting wide open by that same energy. This is the point where your friends need to slow down their drumming to the same rate as your resting heartbeat.

Brainwave Entrainment Audios

Another great way to facilitate your quest is to use brainwave entrainment audio. Brainwave entrainment is also called brainwave synchronization. It is the process of generating specific brainwave frequencies in you, using a stimulus that matches the frequencies of the brain state you want to achieve.

Your brain has a habit of adjusting its main electroencephalographic frequency when there's a strong enough stimulus, which in this case would be sound. So, rather than go for regular music, you can up your chances by using music specifically created with brainwave entrainment audio. Think of it as a shortcut to getting to the astral plane. Of course, this doesn't mean you don't have to do any work focusing, but you'll surely have an easier go of leaving your body.

The following are brainwave entrainment audios worth looking at:

Binaural beats: this audio has two different signals on the left and right, which cause your brain to adjust its frequency accordingly. These signals or tones are long, continuous sounds on their own. However, when you put the headphones on, they generate a new tone, which is the beat itself. It sounds like you hear a steady, percussive beat, but you're not. It is your brain that combines both continuous sounds into a pulsing one. If you've got a tone of 505 Hertz in one ear and 495 Hertz in the other, you'll get a 10 Hertz tone, which is subsonic and is at the midpoint of the Alpha range of frequencies. Playing binaural beats with loudspeakers converts them to monaural beats, so you need headphones to use them effectively.

Monaural beats: these make use of a steadily pulsing single beat. It sounds like a pulse or click when it's in music because two tones from a single speaker come together. You don't need headphones for monaural beats, and in fact, they are a lot more effective than binaural beats. They tend to interfere with music unpleasantly, so it's best to use them on their own if that bothers you.

Isochronic beats: these are a form of monaural beats. They are single tones, but they're different from monaural beats because they have a sine wave pulse instead of a single tone with separate pulses. In English: isochronic tones are sounds that come on and off in a steady rhythm. This constant switch between "on" and "off" is what influences your brain to change its frequencies. You can play isochronic beats with your loudspeaker and still reap the full benefits.

Sound and light entrainment: this uses sound and light machines, or mind machines, if you will. The audio used with this form of entrainment includes monaural, binaural, and isochronic beats. They are a lot more powerful than audio beats independently, and they act a lot faster. You also work with glasses with diodes in them or a computer screen that shows you lights that flash in sync with the audio. Again, this is pretty powerful stuff, so don't jump right to this without checking out the other forms of entrainment. Also, use this with caution.

There are other forms of brainwave entrainment, but we're keeping our focus on what works along with music and mantras, so this is all you need to know.

Mantras

One of the most crucial requirements for mastering astral projection is raising your resting awareness level. You want to master the art of being in a state of complete rest, in body and mind, while being fully aware of what's happening, instead of drifting off to sleep on account of exhaustion or boredom. Fortunately, if you can learn any skill, you can learn this one too. A great way to speed up your learning process is by using music and mantras. The cool thing about using these tools is that they not only boost your resting level of awareness but can help with leaving your body directly from waking consciousness.

A mantra is any word or sentence that you say either mentally or aloud, over and over again. Mantras can either be meaningless or hold meaning. For astral projection, you will find it best to stick with mantras that mean something to you and keep the language positive. As always, word your mantras in the present tense, not the past or present continuous, or future tenses.

Mantras aren't an English concept. However, that doesn't mean a mantra in English is any less potent than one in Sanskrit. Remember, the true power lies not in the word itself but the meaning you ascribe to it. So, you can boost your awareness right now with a mantra perfectly worded for your intentions.

Getting in the right frame of mind for astral projection is easy and challenging to do with mantras. You don't need to think too long and hard about them, and there are no steps for you to recall, so that's the easy part. The hard part is keeping yourself on the razor-thin edge of being awake and asleep.

When you've settled on a mantra, you must remember that you can't just repeat it mindlessly. You have to do so with full awareness, backing it up with your willpower. You can think of this as an exercise in concentration. You've got to keep your attention squarely on the meaning of your mantra. Ideally, make a habit of doing this each night, and you will reap the rewards.

To use your mantra, make sure you're in a very comfortable sleeping position so you have no reason to move or fidget. For example, if you're a bit overweight, you may snore if you lie on your back, and that sound will distract you. The best thing to do in this case is to lie on your left side for good results. Then, when you're sure that you're very comfortable and will have no reason to move, you can begin with the mantra.

Using Your Mantra

Start by chanting your chosen mantra out loud, and then as you grow more relaxed, chant it in your mind. As you repeat this mantra, dwell on its meaning. Don't be surprised if you get a successful astral projection out of it right away. This is such a powerful astral projection technique, if done right. If you're struggling to find a good mantra, you can just go with this simple one: *I am awake and aware in every realm.*

You must think about the words you're saying as you use the mantra to grow the ability of your conscious mind to maintain its awareness and grow stronger in focus. If you repeat them mindlessly, you'll be strengthening your subconscious mind—which is almost a pointless thing to do since it's already mighty.

When you've repeated your mantra enough times, you'll most likely notice you're falling asleep. You might find your words hang or slur, or you say something else. Hearing this shouldn't discourage you. It means you're aware you're falling asleep, which is good. All you need to do is resume chanting the mantra. In the process, you'll maintain that balance between sleep and wakefulness. You'll learn how to trick your body into assuming you're fast asleep when your mind is wide awake.

Don't just use your mantra when you want to astral travel. Instead, you should use it daily to increase your ability to remain aware at rest and throughout your day. Sit in a comfy chair, or a stool, or on the floor if you like, and then chant your mantra for ten to fifteen minutes.

Mantras for Astral Projection

Thanks to Samael Aun Weor's Gnostic teachings, there are so many mantras you can use to leave your body, each of them as powerful as the rest. Here's how to pronounce the vowels in these mantras:

- *A* as in "alpha."
- *E* as in "left."
- *I* and *Y* as in "thief."
- *O* as in "core."
- *U* as in "choose."

Now let's get on to the mantras.

La Ra: Samael talks about this mantra as he wrote about the Chapultepec temple in the 4th dimension in *The Greater Mysteries* (1956) book. He said all you have to do is chant the mantra in your mind while paying attention to the particularly high-pitched sound within, almost like a cricket. This is the internal sound. You need to be tired and able to hold your mind awake.

Done right, as soon as you enter the trance state, you will feel that sharp cricket sound in your head. What you need to do is lull yourself a bit deeper into sleep and then get up from your bed with your intention front and center in your mind.

Tai Re Re Re: you can lull yourself to sleep with this one. It works pretty well for those who tend to fall asleep as soon as their heads hit the pillow. Chant this in a sing-song manner, emphasizing the A in Tai. The three Resounds are to be strung together in a way that makes it melodious, like a ringing bell. Don't roll the Rs. Tai is to be chanted on a deeper, lower note than the rest of the mantra.

Fa Ra On: this is from the word "Pharaoh." Samael teaches that you must relax and then use the mantra. You can say it out loud in the beginning and then make it softer and softer. Finally, let the chanting become purely mental. As you chant this, envision the Great Pyramid of Egypt—only if you want to. *Egypt* is yet another mantra connected to ancient Egypt if you're interested in exploring that time and place or learning from temples.

Rustic: Samael says you should lie horizontally on your bed and allow your body to relax, so there's no tension on the astral body from the physical one. Chant this in your mind and observe yourself as you fall asleep. Allow yourself to go drowsy as you chant the mantra this way: Ruuuuuuusssstiiii.

When you notice you're on that razor edge, get out of bed and leave your room. Don't overthink the process of leaving your bed, and it will be a lot easier for you to leave your physical body. Assume it requires effort, and you'll have a hard time going.

S: this mantra is easy because all you need to do is make the "S" sound in an exhausted state. When you're in the void, all you need to do is get up and out of bed. When you get out of bed, do so with the same attitude you used to roll out of bed when you knew nothing of astral projection. It's not a mind thing but is just the action of you getting up.

You now have an assortment of mantras to work with that will help you get to the astral plane.

Chapter Twelve: The Meditation Method

Relaxing is probably the most challenging part of astral projection for a lot of people. We all have stressors to deal with each day, at work, school, and at home. If you have mental health issues, then being able to relax might be doubly hard for you. Stress is a factor that makes it hard for us to function correctly in our day-to-day lives, so of course, it stands to reason that it would make it harder to astral project as well. Instead of resorting to harmful drugs, you should consider taking your daily "meds"—by which I mean, meditate daily.

The National Center for Complementary and Integrative Health says that meditation involves both body and mind. Historically, this practice has been used to boost physical relaxation and mental calmness, giving a balanced mind, better health, and general well-being. It's not a new practice at all. Buddhism and similar cultures are all about the process of becoming enlightened using meditation. They have practiced all kinds of meditation for hundreds of years.

Why You Should Meditate

Meditation will help you alleviate stress, which is a huge deal because when your body and mind are chronically stressed, your body's telomeres become shorter. Telomeres are responsible for keeping your body's chromosomes intact. If they fade away, your chromosomes will break down, and this will cause weakness in your bones and immune system, among other things. In June 2016, ScienceDirect published a study that shows that regular meditation reduces stress and inflammatory response to chemical *and* psychological sources of stress over the long term. This means you get to live longer and healthier.

You didn't pick up this book to learn to be healthier, though. You want to have astral projections. Meditation helps you with the process because constant practice will reveal to you the actual nature of reality. The more you meditate, the more paranormal experiences you will have, which will show you that life isn't quite what it seems and that the power is within you to be, do, and have it all. You will find your mind becoming more open and accepting of the truth about our multidimensional existence, understanding that the physical world is barely the tip of the iceberg. This is the right mindset to have towards spiritual matters like astral projection.

Astral projection requires mastery of the mind, and you'll find there's no better way to take charge of your thoughts and emotions than by practicing meditation. The more you meditate, the more fearless you become. You rid your subconscious mind of all the phobias, addictions, depression, and anxiety that stops you from leaving your body.

Here are more reasons to meditate:

1. Meditation helps you build your brain so that you're happier, less stressed, more successful, and have stellar memory. It also makes it easier for you to fall asleep (while

keeping your mind alert), helps with learning, and improves your emotional and intelligence quotients.

2. It balances both hemispheres of your brain so that your brain is wholly synchronized, which leads to fantastic creativity and insight, as well as better mental health.

3. You can boost your serotonin, endorphins, and other chemicals while reducing cortisol, the stress hormone.

4. Look younger than you really are and feel that way without the need for expensive beauty products or excessive supplements.

5. Trying to lose weight? Accelerate the process with meditation. *The Journal of Obesity* (Robinson et al.) looked into the connection between weight loss and body image, working with 14,000 adults. They found that those who thought of themselves as fat were likely to put on weight in the future. Researchers from the UCLA school of medicine found that meditation improves the region of your brain responsible for being compassionate to yourself to stop thinking of yourself as overweight. As a result, you lose fat.

6. The world's most successful people often attribute their success to meditation.

7. Your intuition improves the more you meditate, along with your mental toughness, grit, and happiness.

8. If you have insomnia, consider making meditation a practice in your life.

Preparing to Project Using Meditation

Before you start, you need to make sure you prepare yourself. You may find at the beginning that you have issues with remaining in a meditative state for extended periods since this isn't usual for you. Still, you can set things up, so your session goes relatively well anyway.

First, you have to get rid of all distractions. If you've got a pet, get someone to take care of them or put them in a different room and close the door. If you've got kids and they're at an age where getting them to quiet down is a Herculean feat, then you can practice this when it's nap time or have them go on a play date. You could also give them something to occupy their attention.

Put your phone on silent mode or turn it off completely. If you want to receive calls from certain people, you can set your phone up to ring only when they call you, so you're available in case of an emergency.

Turn the lights down low in the room to a comfortable degree, so you're not distracted by the light, and you're not worried about it being too dark. If you want to, you can use scented candles to set the mood and make your room nice and warm as well. Speaking of setting the mood, you can play some soothing meditation music. You'll find great meditation playlists on Spotify or YouTube.

Do you live in a noisy place? Then you can turn up the volume of your meditation music or use your headphones. The best kind of music is the sort without drums, something easy going that makes you feel at peace. If you're going to meditate without music, you can just use earplugs. Investing in a white noise machine is not a bad idea either. It will get rid of the noise from your neighbors, as well as traffic and electrical appliances like your fridge.

Make sure you're as comfortable as can be. For this, wear loose clothing, and keep your room at the perfect temperature, so you don't have to interrupt your trip just because it's too hot or cold. Another thing to pay attention to is how you're sitting. Make sure you won't get pins and needles over time. Finally, whatever you do, don't lie down, especially when you're just starting out. If not, you might fall asleep.

Robert Monroe's Meditation Method for Astral Projection

Robert Monroe is a legend in the field of astral travel. Here's his method for astral projection through a meditation-induced trance state.

1. **Relax.** Your body and mind need to be at ease. Use the progressive relaxation method by scanning your body from your feet, calves, thighs, torso, and arms to your neck and head. If you feel a bit of tension anywhere, breathe it out. You can scan your body several times till you feel you're ready for the next step.

2. **Get into a trance state.** Stay still, keep your eyes shut, ignore all impulses to turn and scratch any itches. Count from 300 to 1 to keep your mind alert while your body falls asleep. Remember, it's alright if you lose count. You can just start over.

3. **Induce the vibrations.** To do this, Monroe suggests you should imagine you're already vibrating. Feel the vibrations in your mind, and they will come.

4. **Own the vibrations.** Play with stopping and restarting them, so you know you're the captain of this astral ship. You can control them with simple intention and sensation.

5. **Imagine you're separating.** Remain fully aware of the thought of your astral body leaving the physical. Concentration is key. If your thoughts drift off, you will lose control and have to begin the process again.

6. **Dissociate the astral body from the physical one.** You can do this by imagining you're getting lighter and lighter, so light that you float up and out of your body with ease. If you find this hard to do, then Monroe suggests you practice a partial separation. Push your astral foot or hand through

your wall or floor, and then pull it back into your regular body.

You might be wondering, where exactly is the meditation in all of this? Anytime you have to fix your awareness on something, whether it's an object, a sensation, your breath, or the mind-awake-body-asleep state, you're actually meditating. Progressive relaxation is a form of meditation. Mindfulness is another form, and the successful astral traveler knows how important it is for you to mind your mind.

Entering a Deep Meditative State

To get into deep meditation, you need to warm up properly. In other words, you must be completely relaxed. Deep breathing is essential. You should also make sure your head is in the right space, and your intention to go deep into meditation is clear and strong.

Various meditation methods will have their own unique effects on your mind, depending on how deep you allow yourself to go. Usually, you'll find yourself immersed in a sea of calmness, with your focus clear and your entire being centered on the here and now. As a result, you'll feel a sense of contentment, clarity, and complete awareness.

Before You Go Deep

First things first, slow your breath and relax your body. Your breath, body, and mind are all connected. When you breathe slower and deeper, you calm your mind, and your body unwinds. Your parasympathetic nervous system kicks in, and your stress response goes down.

Make sure you're wearing loose, comfy clothing. Sit in a chair or on a comfortable cushion and shut your eyes. Breathe in through your nose and then out through your slightly parted lips. That's one breath cycle. Repeat this twice more, or up to five times if that helps you relax better. Make your breaths deep and even. You'll notice the exhale is longer than the inhale. This is fine.

As you breathe in, feel yourself rooted to the present, fully aware of the here and now. On your exhale, allow your body to relax fully, releasing all tension in all the muscles. Pay attention to your forehead, tongue, throat, and jaw. These places tend to carry tension, so make sure to relax them consciously.

Enter a state of joy and contentment. You want to make sure this is how you feel before you meditate. This tells your mind that everything is okay, and there's no need to hop from thought to thought in restlessness. You can recall something you're thankful for or how great it feels to meditate if you have experience with that. If you're religious, you can say a short prayer to your deity before you meditate. This will further center your focus and give you the sense of sacredness needed to make this a fruitful experience. Feel love and thankfulness that you're learning to heal your mind and grow in your mastery of this fantastic tool.

State your intention. With full awareness of the meaning of your words, state your intention, which is what you want to get out of this deep meditative state. For example, you may intend to increase your resting awareness level or gain access to unique insights that will shift your life to the next level. It helps to add a statement like this: "For the next ten minutes, I focus my full attention on my meditation. I have nothing to do and nothing to think of at this time. Mind be at peace. I will attend to all thoughts after my meditation. I will begin my focus, now."

Choose something to place your awareness on. It could be your breath, candlelight, or a spot on the wall. It doesn't matter what you choose, as long as you keep your awareness trained on it. You could focus on any of your chakras or all of them. You could simply sit with the awareness of your higher self or guide being with you. You could keep your mind focused on the memory of your vibrating body as you meditate. The choices are endless and all up to you.

Go easy on yourself when distracted—*no matter how often you lose focus.* If you beat yourself up each time you get distracted, then you've lost the essence of deep meditation, to begin with. Even if your mind strays a thousand times a minute, *go easy on yourself.* You should know it's a great thing you keep catching your mind as it wanders because it signifies that your awareness is improving. Higher awareness will do wonders for your meditation and astral projection. You have spent many years being distracted, so don't expect that's a habit you can undo with a Thanos snap.

Enjoy the process of being focused. There will be times during your meditation where your awareness is laser-sharp. Enjoy this. Enjoy the quietness in your mind. This teaches it to seek out more of it, reinforcing your new routine of daily deep meditation. The more you actively choose to enjoy the meditation, the less your mind will reach out to think mundane, filler thoughts to stuff the silence with.

Transition gently out of deep meditation. Choose a soft-sounding alarm to bring you out of your meditative state. Come back to everyday waking awareness slowly, gently. Don't be in a hurry. You'll know when the time is right to open your eyes. When you move between states gently, you'll cause the meditative state of mind to bleed into other aspects of your life.

Journal. You should take notes of your practice. Note the time and place and how you felt. If you got any insights at all as you meditated, you should write them down too. Write down how long you meditated, how you feel after meditation, and what state your mind was in during the process. The last item includes details about how often you grew distracted and the kinds of thoughts and sensations or emotions that distracted you. Note how long, on average, you were able to keep your focus.

Note that if you want to leave your body when you're in deep meditation, you can. Simply imagine your chakras opening up, and then imagine you can feel the intense but pleasant vibrations take over your entire form. Then, when you're in complete control of the vibrations, you may stand and leave in your astral form.

If you want to take meditation up a notch, you should try to meditate in the astral realm. Keep in mind you won't be there long if you just sit still. To remain in meditation in the astral plane for longer, keep up a rapid, continuous motion with your astral hands. You can rub them vigorously together, so you last longer in that state. Meditating in the astral realm will have very potent effects on your waking life. Don't be surprised when you start experiencing more synchronicity and other paranormal events in your life. It's all good stuff, as long as you don't respond with fear.

Chapter Thirteen: The Wake-Back-to-Bed Method

The Wake-Back-to-Bed method, also called WBTB, is a very effective way to leave your body, which is why it's so popular. Initially, it was used for inducing lucidity in dreams. Still, you can use it for astral projection as well, either from a dream or from waking reality.

This technique is often used along with others. It is the foundation that lucid dreamers and astral projectors work with when experimenting with other methods or exercises for the astral plane. The point is to make sure you are very alert before you go back to bed. Since you've already had some sleep, you don't have to worry about being too tired to keep your mind focused on your intention to visit the astral realm.

Before Using This Method

You're more likely to succeed with this only if you're already familiar with becoming lucid in your dreams and remaining in control of them. Like astral projection, this is a skill that will take practice, dedication, and time. You can have a lucid dream on your first try, but you should set realistic expectations.

Record your dreams in a journal. This is one of the first and best things to do. You should keep a dream journal, which will serve as subconscious reinforcement that it matters for you to remember your dreams. Just recording them, even if you only remember one image, will boost your dream recall dramatically. Dream recall is crucial because it will give you the control and calm you need when you realize you're in a dream and when you astral project. So, make a point of writing your dreams down each time you wake up.

Reality checks. A reality check is just a test you do in your waking life to be sure you're wide awake and not just in a very vivid dream or something. You can set the alarm to go off randomly to perform these checks, and you should also do them as they occur to you. First, you will test your reality to see if the customary laws of waking life still hold. If you notice there's something off, chances are you're dreaming. The more you do them, the more you'll train your mind to ask constantly, "Am I dreaming?" There can only be one answer when you're awake—and an entirely different one in the dream state.

Every time you notice something strange, do a reality check. This is why reality checks don't work for some people. You shouldn't only check your reality when your alarm goes off. Check it when you notice something strange because dreams tend to have a lot of weird stuff going on, which can trigger you to become lucid if you've been doing your checks the right way. You should do your checks:

- When you hear, see, smell, feel, or taste something unusual.

- When you're doing nothing, just looking around the place.

- When you come face to face with one of your dream signs.

- At random intervals.

- When you look in the mirror, if you're dreaming, you'll see something weird.

- You can check every hour on the hour.

- When you look at your watch or your ring, if you have one. (Consider getting a dream totem ring to remind you to do your checks when you see it).

- Every time you see the letter "A" on the back of your hand. You have to write the letter down.

- When you drink something.

List of Reality Checks

Here are reality checks you can use that will give you outstanding results. Make sure to ask yourself, "Am I dreaming?" as you do each test.

1. Push a finger through your palm. It will go through in a dream. It doesn't hurt, so don't worry.

2. Push your hand through a wall.

3. Check your watch for the time. Look away, and then look back at it. If you're dreaming, it will give a different time or look like gibberish. Skip this if you don't do watches. You can look at your phone's clock instead.

4. Read any text around you, look away, then look back and read again. If it changes, you're dreaming.

5. Ask yourself, "Am I dreaming now?" You can ask in your head or out loud. As you ask, analyze the room you're in. Then, ask yourself how you got there. Work backward by remembering the last thing you did before asking, and the thing before, and on and on. Dreams usually don't have any continuity of events. So if you're dreaming, you'll be able to tell because there's no way you could have made it from Mexico to Paris in two minutes.

6. Ask someone else if you're dreaming. You'll get an interesting answer if you are.

7. Look at your hands. If you're dreaming, they'll look weird. If they don't look strange and you're dreaming, you'll know it anyway.

8. Check your pulse. If you don't have one, you're either a vampire or, more likely, you're dreaming.

9. Put your glasses on or take them off.

10. Look in the mirror.

11. Flip a coin and keep it floating in the air.

12. Jump with the intention to float.

13. Turn a light switch on and off. Switches don't usually work in dreams. Do other checks as well, just in case your dreams have excellent electrical wiring. If not, you might get a false positive, where you assume you're awake.

14. Lift something heavy with no effort.

15. Hold your hand out and will it to stretch to the other side of the room.

16. Stick out your tongue and pull it, so it grows ridiculously long.

17. Look at something made of glass or china and will it to break with your mind.

18. Think of a celebrity and imagine them walking through the door to meet you.

19. Pinch yourself. If you're dreaming, you won't feel any pain.

20. Imagine the floor is lava and wait to see if it changes.

21. Think of a loved one or relative who you know is eons away from you and imagine them coming out of a room in your home.

22. Put your hands together and try to make them melt into one giant fist.

Don't rush through these checks as you do them, or you risk convincing yourself you're awake when you're dreaming. The best checks are the irrefutable ones. For instance, you could never put your finger through your palm, so if you do, then you're in "La La Land." Also, meditate everyday day for ten to fifteen minutes, and make a point of doing your reality checks as soon as you wake up in the morning.

How to Use the WBTB Method

This is the WBTB method adapted to suit astral projection.

Go to bed. Before you do, set the alarm to wake you up after you've had four, maybe five hours of sleep. When it goes off, turn it off and go back to bed. What's the point of this? You want to break the sleep cycle just before you get into the REM stage of sleep. REM is short for "Rapid Eye Movement," which happens every time you dream. Usually, this sleep phase kicks in after about five hours. Still, you should experiment with various timings to find what works best for you. For most people, anywhere from three to five hours of sleep is good enough but find your sweet spot.

Stay awake for a bit. When your alarm wakes you, get out of bed and keep yourself busy for fifteen to ninty minutes. You might need to experiment to find out just how much time works for you. Most people find twenty minutes is more than sufficient. Do what you must to keep your mind active and alert, but don't get so alert that it's difficult for you to go back to sleep. Alternatively, so you don't bore yourself to sleep while waiting, you may read something about astral projection until it's time to go back to sleep.

Go back to bed. This time have a solid intention in your mind that you will recognize you're dreaming when it happens. Let yourself relax and go back to bed. This is when some dreamers choose to add a second method to increase their chances of success, like the IMP method (more on that later).

In your dream, go to your bedroom. When you realize you're dreaming, go to your room (or wherever you know you fell asleep). It doesn't matter where you are; just think about your room, and you'll be right back there. Take a good look at your body and the room as well. Examine it for details which you can check when you wake up. Some say, once you can see your body, and the room feels steady and real (about as "real" as it gets in the astral), then you're out of the body. Others say you need to experience the actual process of separation. I'm of the latter opinion, which is why I've included these extra steps. Better safe than sorry.

Alternatively, plan your exit. Once you've achieved lucidity, fill your mind with the intention to leave your body and plan how you're going to do it. Are you going to roll out or use the rope method? Are you going to allow yourself to float out of your body like a cloud? Is your intention to have your guide help with pulling you out? Also, what are you going to do when out of the body? Plan that out in your lucid dream. Having a plan in place will ensure you don't waste any time when it's time to exit. You won't feel confused or distracted by anything happening in the dream.

Begin to wake up. Again, a simple intention to do so will suffice. You will notice that the waking up process is a lot slower. This will give you all the time you need to remain on that razor edge between waking and sleeping consciousness so that it's super easy for you to exit your body using your preferred method.

Leave your body. When you feel yourself on the bed, just roll out with your astral body. You can also float out if you prefer.

The fantastic thing about the Wake-Back-to-Bed technique is you don't have to go through the process of relaxing your whole body, which is what a lot of folks struggle with. So, if you find that you're constantly falling asleep when you're trying to relax, then give WBTB a whirl.

Lucid Dream or the Astral Realm?

How can you tell the difference between the two? Anyone who has had both experiences will tell you they are two different things. Sure, they have the same element of not taking place in the physical realm and allowing you to create something with pure intention, but that's about it. It's a feeling. One feels more dreamlike, while the other feels more "real," for lack of a better word. It's like comparing the world you see in a virtual reality game to the physical world.

Your dreams are mostly made up of reference material from your waking life; your subconscious mind generates them. It works with everything you've ever witnessed, whether you were conscious of it or not, to create that world. Your dreams are no less powerful just because they're made of subconscious material, though. You can get amazing insight that improves your psyche and will help you do better in waking life. Your dreams reflect all the troubles you go through in the day and feed you with the solution if you ask and keep your eyes open for an answer.

Astral projections are a whole other matter. You're actually leaving your body when you astral project. You enter another dimension of reality entirely, using your astral body. Here are more differences between both states:

You hear voices as you're projecting. This happens because you're between worlds. Even if you're not trying to project, as you fall asleep, you do separate from your body a bit, even if it's only a few inches. You become unaware of your physical body, more focused on your mind, until your attention moves outward when you hear the voices. It could be singing or talking. You won't always hear voices, though. Sometimes it's other sounds, thunder, or the gentle tinkling of delicate bells, or anything else, really.

Lucid dreaming only happens in your sleep state. There's nothing real about the experience. Your consciousness is still with your physical body. To leave your body, however, you cannot be asleep. Instead, your mind remains awake, which means you retain consciousness, and therefore the experience is very real.

You cannot control other beings on the astral plane. It just doesn't work. In a lucid dream, you can get others to do your bidding. After all, they are a reflection of your subconscious, so you're in charge of them. However, astral beings have autonomy. Just like you can't impose your will on others in the physical world, you can't do that in the astral. You can, however, affect some control of your interactions and conversations to a certain extent.

You can't change the environment in the astral realm. Wherever you find yourself, you can't change the setting. It is what it is. In a lucid dream, you'd be able to make night day and vice versa. In the astral, you can't because that realm exists independent to you. You'd have better luck trying to turn the Great Pyramid into the Statue of Liberty in real life than trying to change your environment in the astral plane.

You have to understand the fundamental differences between astral projection and lucid dreaming. If you confuse one for the other, you're likely losing out on the many benefits that both of them can give you. But, again, just because lucid dreaming isn't real doesn't mean it's pointless or has no benefits. You can use the power of your subconscious mind through your lucid dreams to heal yourself and others, come up with unique ideas for business or your next screenplay or painting, work out creative solutions to troubles at work or at home, and so much more.

The feeling of astral projecting is unmistakable, from being in the void to the vibrations and the sensation of the astral you separating from the physical you. If all you've done up to this point is lucid dreams, you will *know* this is a whole other ballgame when you have your first projection. You will have zero doubts in your mind that you're not dreaming because your consciousness is fully present and in control of itself, but not your environment. Also, things tend to be a lot more stable in the astral realm than in your dreams. That's another sure sign to keep in mind.

Chapter Fourteen: Other Astral Projection Techniques

Before using any technique, you should make sure you're in a state of deep trance. Please use the relaxation techniques already mentioned in this book to achieve the trance state before attempting to exit. You can achieve trance through any of the already mentioned exercises in this book. You can also resist the urge you have to move when you wake up in the morning and keep your eyes shut. Do this right, and you might find you're in light sleep paralysis, between the waking world and the dream one.

You can use the relaxation method you're about to read in the first method below for your convenience. Subsequent methods will be written with the assumption that you have adequately relaxed your body and brought your mind into a trance state.

Robert Bruce's Seven-Step Rope Method

The rope method is a straightforward and effective way to come out of your body. It keeps the time needed to leave your body very short. But, before you do this, here's a little exercise:

- Shut your eyes and take a few relaxing breaths.

- In your mind's hands, hold an apple. Feel its shape.

- Now, hold a golf ball. Feel how hard it is. Feel the bumps all over it using your hands.

- Hold a hot potato now. Allow the heat to seep through each palm.

- Hold an ice cube. Rub it all over your hands.

- Now, hold a soccer ball. Feel what it's like in your hands.

- Feel the texture of fur.

- Use your mind's hands to rip a piece of paper to pieces. Feel the sensations with each tear.

Don't skip this exercise because it teaches you how to work with your astral hands, which is a skill that you'll need when you're leaving your body.

Relax. Sit (or lie) in a comfortable position, and then shut your eyes. Breathe in and out, deep and slow. You want to imagine that on every exhale, all the tension in your body melts away. Keep this up until you feel completely at ease. You can use a mantra to help you. Simply saying, "I am very, very relaxed" on each exhale will do. If you had tried to project before and failed to do so with full consciousness each time, you should spend at least thirty minutes relaxing even more.

Get into a trance state. This is the stage between sleep and wakefulness, with your mind very active and aware. If your mind remains active, you don't have to worry too much about totally falling asleep. Instead, you can use the counting process or a mantra.

Slip deeper into relaxation. Keeping your eyes closed, look into the darkness. You will see patterns pop up in your line of sight. Pay them no mind, and they'll go away. With time, you will notice you can't feel your body anymore. Don't panic. Sleep paralysis is a good thing.

On to the vibrations. This can be pretty hard for beginning astral travelers to achieve, but it is doable. All you need to do is imagine or feel your energy centers or chakras vibrating with energy, being filled with light to make the vibrations come. Try not to overdo this. They may start in just one body part. If this happens, putting your attention on them should make them more intense, and then you can move them around your body. As you do this, the vibrations will begin.

Control your vibrations. With your intention, play with the vibrations by increasing their frequency. For example, you can slow them down to a stop and then start them up again, or you can speed them up until they hit a very fine, high frequency. When you feel like you are in complete control of the vibrations, you can move on to the next step.

Use the rope. Imagine that there's a rope hanging right over you, just within reach. With your eyes still closed and your body still, imagine yourself reaching out for this rope and then grabbing it. Next, pull your astral self out of the physical body. The first couple of times you try this, you should only pull yourself partway out and allow your astral body to return to the physical one briefly. Do this enough times until you feel like you're in complete control of your astral body.

Separate yourself. When you've proven you're in control through the partial separation step, it's time to head out. Just pull your entire astral body out, putting one hand over the other on the rope until you've left your body. It helps if you chant in your mind or set the intention, "Light as a feather." This way, you don't take on the idea that it should be harder to pull yourself out because you erroneously assume the astral body is heavy like the physical one.

You'll know it's working when you get a feeling of vertigo in your chest and stomach. This is caused by the pressure of this method on your astral body. Continue to climb, and you will soon be out. It's essential to remain physically relaxed and mentally calm. You can practice using the rope right now before you're ready to project, so you know what to expect. Use your imagination and your memory of ropes to help you generate the natural sensation of climbing.

The IMP Method

IMP is short for "Impossible Movement Practice." The point is to attempt to do movements that are physically impossible in waking reality. The best kinds of movements are the subtle ones. However, you can be more ambitious. For example, bend your leg entirely backward from the middle of your thigh or bend your arm at the forearm (in real life, the only bending would happen at the elbow). Pick movements that wouldn't work in real life for you because of a different body part that makes it impossible.

Choose the movement you prefer, and then in your mind, repeat it over and over from the first-person point of view. Feel the chosen body part bending and moving in the most ridiculous of ways. Eventually, this sensation will go from imagined to tangible on an astral level. You will begin to feel vibrations. You can then allow the movement to transition into your astral body separating from your physical one.

The Free Fall Method

See yourself falling down swiftly. Imagine all the sensations that come with falling. Feel how fast you're falling and feel yourself tumbling over and over. If you do this right, you will feel the vibrations, and you'll get a weird sense of not knowing exactly where you are in terms of space. When you notice voices, buzzing sounds, vibrations, and your heart beating faster, just keep going with your visualization. When you notice you're close to projecting, imagine hitting the ground suddenly. This sudden collision with the ground will trigger a separation from your body.

The Yo-Yo Method

Just before you get in bed to go to sleep, pick a spot in your room that you're familiar with, whether it's your closet, door, bookshelf, or lamp. When you've chosen a location, examine it thoroughly. Notice all the details you can about what it looks like. Touch all the areas of that spot, memorize all the tactile sensations you get, and then go to bed. As soon as you're awake, move your consciousness straight to the area you studied before. Imagine it as vividly as you can for just one second, then return your awareness to the darkness behind your eyes for one second. The next second, shift your attention to the spot you've visualized and then back to the darkness after that. The yo-yo effect of moving from point to point in focus will trigger vibrations and complete separation from the physical body.

The Listening Method

Focus on the sounds inside your head when you're in the trance state. You'll notice humming, buzzing, or voices. Whatever you hear, just continue to listen, even when the intensity and volume of the sounds increase. When the sounds get really loud, use a rapid movement to separate from your body. You might find the sounds have already pulled you out into the astral plane on their own.

The Exhaustion Method

It's so easy to fall asleep when you're exhausted. The trick, then, is to find a way to keep your mind awake while your body shuts down. Considering how tired your body is, you will naturally be very relaxed, allowing you to get into sleep paralysis quickly.

Don't go to bed to use this method until you find it incredibly difficult to keep your eyes open. Next, you want to lie down somewhere uncomfortable or in an awkward position. If you're too comfy, you just might let your mind drift to sleep as well. So, if you're a belly or side sleeper, lie on your back. If you love lying on your back, try your left side.

Remain aware of all the sensations that come with falling asleep. Maintain your awareness, and don't let it fade away. Feel free to exert mental effort in this case because your body will still fall asleep no matter how much is going on in your head.

After the vibration stage with the hypnagogic sensations, get up without using your physical muscles. You will enter the astral realm.

The Forced Sleep Method

Use this one in the morning, right after you wake up. Let your eyes stay closed, and don't move. Don't concentrate on anything either. Allow yourself to sleep for ten seconds. After the ten seconds are up, aggressively separate your astral body from your physical one. This way, your brain is tricked into assuming you're actually going back to bed and will create sleep paralysis, which allows you to astral project easily.

The Rotation Method

Imagine and feel your body rotating about an axis. Do this with no tension in your body. When the rotating motion goes from only being imaginary to feeling real, or you notice your body vibrating, you should intensify the sensations you get. You might hear loud buzzing or notice your heartbeat is a little too fast. Ignore that. Just continue with the rotation, and soon you will find it easy to get out of your body.

The Body Strain Method

This method calls for strain in your entire body without using the muscles. It may sound weird, but you should give this a go. All you have to do is generate a feeling of tension inside your body. This tension isn't physical, just so you know. You will feel a slight electrical current running through you, which can intensify to become the vibrations you get before projection. You can do this once you enter sleep paralysis or right when you wake up. Strain your astral body, and notice what happens next. You should get a feeling of floating, as well as the vibrations and weird sounds. Continue to strain until you're out.

The Brain Strain Method

Generate that same straining sensation from the previous method within your brain. Imagine the feeling of your brain being squeezed in your head. You will feel a non-physical tension, which will lead to vibrations and a feeling of vertigo. Continue to strain your brain till you attain complete separation.

The Running Method

When you have accomplished the trance state, or just after you've woken up from sleep, vividly feel yourself running very fast while keeping your physical muscles relaxed. You don't have to be able to visualize yourself running. The simple sensation of running will do. Keep going faster and faster, and you will get the vibrations. When the vibrations are very intense, imagine a solid wall just up ahead, and run towards it even quicker. When you smack the wall, you will trigger a separation from your physical body.

The Tunnel Method

Imagine a tunnel, long and dark. You're standing in it. Imagine that at the end of this tunnel is a bright light. Fly through the tunnel, feeling the sensation of flight as fully as you can. If it helps, you can generate the same feeling you do in an airplane just before take-off. Go through this tunnel with increasing speed, and soon you'll feel the vibrations and hear noises as well. Ignore both and keep your attention on the light at the end of the tunnel. Once you arrive at the white light, your astral body will separate from the physical, and you can begin your journey.

The Third Eye Method

You're going to need your third eye for this one. You can find it in between your eyes, just slightly above the eyebrows. That's the seat of your consciousness. For this projection method, you must keep your focus on this spot. Turn your physical eyes toward the third eye and keep all of your attention there. With time, you will notice the vibrations and a floating feeling. Keep your awareness there until you feel completely separate from the physical.

The Swimming Method

If you swim well, then all you need to make this work is muscle memory. When you're in a trance, imagine the sensation of swimming as vividly as you can. Remember what it feels like to be in the water and move just like that in your mind while keeping your physical muscles relaxed and motionless. You'll get the same effect as the rope technique, with the gradual increase in vibrations that lead to a complete separation.

The Eye Movement Method

This is excellent for causing the vibrations or intensifying them. When you're in the perfect state, all you have to do is move your eyes behind your lids from left to right, back and forth. The result is your focal point will be thrown off balance, and this will deepen the vibrations, leading to a projection.

The Wiggling Method

For this, just wiggle your hands or feet while keeping them relaxed and still. You're working with the astral body here. When the feelings go from imagination to actual astral sensations, that means you're on your way to leaving your body. Continue to wiggle, moving that sensation from just the hands or feet to other parts of your body. Imagine that the wiggling feeling is loosening up your astral body, prying it from the physical. Keep this up until you're out.

The Recall Method

This one works best for those who have already projected before. Imagine your previous astral projection as vividly as you can when you're in the sleep paralysis stage. Bring to mind the sights and sounds, all the sensations that came along with it. Make it as vivid as you can. Remember what it was like to leave your body. Include all the details in your recollection, like the vibrations, sounds, feelings of heaviness, and so on. As you do this, you will inevitably project.

The Room Method

Imagine you're walking around or standing in the same room you're sleeping in from the trance state. If you prefer, you could pick a different room. When I want to make sure I find myself out of body outside the house, I like to choose a location with lots of open space, like on a hill. You want to make sure you imagine you're where you are from a first-person perspective. In other words, you should be looking *through* your own eyes around the room and not looking at yourself as though you're an actor on a movie screen or something.

Feel your feet firmly connected with the floor. If you have a rug in your room, allow your toes to really sink into the material and feel it. Continue to visualize this until it feels more real than you being in bed. What this does is shift your consciousness away from your body. This is a very effective method and I can't recommend it enough.

The Backflip Method

When you wake up, try to do a backflip without moving your physical body. Unfortunately, this will cause your point of consciousness to shift so dramatically that you'll immediately be out of your body. If you have trouble with this, you should spend more time getting deeper into relaxation or trying a different method.

The Levitation Method

In sleep paralysis, or just as you awaken from a dream, immediately levitate out of your body. You must do this with a confident attitude as if you've always done this your whole life. Don't think about it, just do it. At this point, you should know that your physical body isn't supposed to move. This method will help you move to the astral plane right away, or it will at least get you closer to your exit.

The Roll Out Method

From trance or as soon as you wake up, immediately roll out of your body just the way you would in waking life if you were rolling out of bed. Remain relaxed physically while you aggressively roll your astral body out.

The Train Method

Imagine being on a high-speed train, running through its corridor to the other end. Hear the noise the train makes. This will trigger the auditory hypnagogia that accompanies astral projections. Running through the train, continue to focus on the noise and allow it to build up in intensity. At the end of the train, jump off. When you hit the ground, you will leave your body.

The Hammock Method

Imagine you're swinging in a hammock. Make the swinging sensation as natural as you can. Let the hammock swing you higher and higher and allow your astral senses to match those feelings. Eventually, you will get vibrations and hear sounds. To leave your body, simply fall off the hammock as you hit the highest point in the air.

Combining Methods

For best results, you can combine methods. Here is a list of combinations for you to try:

- The WBTB method works great with the IMP technique.

- The rope method goes very well with the third eye method.

- Use the body strain or brain strain method along with the forced sleep technique.

- Use the wiggle to lead into the rope, levitation, or backflip methods.

- The exhaustion technique works with just about any other one.

- The listening method can and should be incorporated with others for extra oomph and a successful astral projection.

Chapter Fifteen: You're There. Now What?

Congratulations on finally making it to the astral realm. You may not have had an easy go of it, but it does get better and easier with time. When you've got the learning curve over and done with, you can now truly begin to explore all the beautiful things in store for you on this plane. You'll get to experience self-healing, transmutation, communing with spirits and other beings, getting information about the past, present, and future, as well as alternate dimensions of reality.

Before you do all of this, you need to learn three basic things:

- How to solidify your experience.

- How to extend the duration of your stay in the astral plane.

- How to navigate the space.

With a complete understanding of the basics, you will stay fully aware of the astral realm. Your sensory faculties will be extremely sharp, and your environment will be as stable for as long as you need it to be.

Solidifying Your Experience

You stand to gain a lot from thoroughly grounding your senses and self-awareness in the astral realm. Ideally, you should always solidify your experience. Do this as soon as you have separated from your body or right after attaining lucidity in your dream. Solidifying your lucidity is one way to make sure you do not lose consciousness of the fact that you're astral projecting. Sometimes, you enter the astral plane with full awareness, which leads to a steady, stable environment. Other times though, that's not the case. This will affect how long you can remain in that realm and how intense the entire journey is for you.

According to Raduga, the best way to create this solidification is through sensory amplification. This entails making the astral realm as physical as possible, allowing the quality of "realness" to fully manifest wherever you find yourself. The way to make this happen is to tune your senses to all the stimuli from the astral environment.

When you leave your body, your sense perception can be very dull. You might find your vision is too blurry or completely absent. Your sense of touch is there, but barely. This is a problem that also affects lucid dreamers the moment they realize they're dreaming. When your senses are dull, there's nothing to see or do, or you misinterpret the sensations you have, and that forces you to go back into your body. Trying to hold on to anything feels like trying to "keep a wave upon the sand." It all just disintegrates. To avoid this, you solidify your experience by amplifying your senses so that you have clarity in sight and touch.

The Other Senses in Solidification

We're not going to dwell on any other senses besides touch and sight because those two are the most important for sensory amplification. Of both senses, touch is the more universal and primitive one. As such, the first sense to work within sensory amplification is the tactile-kinesthetic one. Then, when you are grounded in the environment through touch, you'll find the other senses fix themselves (usually). It's how you can establish that you are in an actual space and not just a floating point of consciousness in the physical world.

Palpation and Peering

To solidify your environment through touch:

As soon as you leave your body, you should grab, rub, or skim the surface features of your environment. This is called *palpation.* Your vision may be useless at this point, but you'll be able to feel surfaces, objects, and other features of your surroundings. These features may or may not be familiar to you, but the more you touch them, the harder and more physical they will feel. You want to make sure you don't leave your hands on any surface or object for longer than a second, or else you will get the sense that it's all dissipating.

Rub your hands together. Doing this is a great way to make your astral body even more physical, in the same way that palpation causes the environment to become more stable. Both palpation and hand rubbing are very effective. You have to do them very deliberately, intensely, almost in a frenzy.

When it comes to vision, you might find it flooding in as soon as you begin touching things. However, palpation and hand rubbing by themselves might not work or might only restore blurry vision. This is because sight can be very slow and stubborn.

To solidify your environment through sight:

Hold up various objects about four to six inches away from your face, and glance at each one quickly. This will cause everything to become brighter and give you more visual focus. This solidification technique is called *peering.*

You can also look at your hands and get into the details you notice. Studying your hands intensely will trigger full vision in about three to ten seconds. Ensure you keep shifting your focus all around as you analyze your hands or the objects around you. If you stare too long at one spot, dissipation will occur.

Use both peering and palpation to help you solidify your experience, especially if you use the same objects or features of your surroundings. Alternating this with rubbing your hands, you will find great success.

Critical Solidification Methods

Now, it's entirely possible that even after all your attempts to bring your environment into complete focus, you still won't be able to perceive much. If this is the case, you should try the following:

1. Strain your body and/or your brain, as described in the previous chapter.

2. Spin quickly and with force. You want to spin around the head-to-toe axis like you're doing cartwheels.

3. Flail about in a very aggressive manner, exaggerating your movements, fully intending to have a clear and complete perception of your environment.

4. Dive to the floor headfirst.

The latter technique might seem a tad much, but it works pretty well. Just dive into the ground, headfirst, flying downwards. After anywhere from five to fifteen seconds, you will find yourself in a brand new environment or a dead end. Don't worry if you notice that doing this dive causes you to lose even more sensory faculties. What you're really doing is returning into the state in between sleep and wakefulness to get to a deeper level of trance before coming back into the astral plane. So don't think it weird if you find you're in a black, blank, or otherwise featureless space while you dive. We have Michael Raduga to thank for this discovery.

Whatever solidification process you use, do it deliberately, aggressively, and continuously to have a successful astral projection. Keep in mind that you're transferring all your senses from your physical body to the astral one. So, it makes sense that your astral body has its senses numb and dull at the start. So, the more force and aggression you use in your movements, peering, and palpation, the more you will embody your astral self and stabilize your environment.

Extending Your Stay in the Astral Realm

The longer you're in the astral, the higher the chances it will all dissipate. To make it last, you want to be aware long enough to at least carry out one of your plans. Fortunately, once you've got the hang of solidification, you will find it easier to extend your stay in the astral. Here's how:

1.Periodically practice peering and palpation as you go about your business in the astral realm. Don't do this the whole time you're there. Do it only every now and then, even if it doesn't seem like your experience will dissipate. If you do notice sudden dissipation, you can try the other techniques besides peering and palpation.

2.Maintain the vibrations. The pulsing, vibratory feeling you have should be kept alive. You can amplify the vibrations by straining your body or your brain. However, suppose at any point you notice that the vibratory sensation is fading. In that case, that means things are about to dissipate, and you should perform one of the critical solidification processes.

3.Examine how aware you are every so often. In other words, you want to keep checking in with yourself to make sure you're conscious you're in an astral projection and you remember exactly why you're there. This way, you'll keep your mind from drifting back into dream consciousness.

4.Don't be spontaneous. Seriously, if you didn't plan something, then don't do it. When you do something that isn't in line with your intentions for that astral trip, you might cause your lucidity and mental acuity to go way down. Then you'll lose yourself in the experience, forgetting you're not dreaming. When anything unexpected makes its way into your environment, do the best you can to make it a part of your action plan. Suppose your goal was to visit an ancient temple to learn the secrets of wealth, but some weird, scary-looking being suddenly accosts you. You can tell it you're in a hurry, and it can either come along or play with you later. Even if the creature seems malevolent, don't be hostile to it, or you'll get the same treatment. Choose to be politely firm when you run into other beings.

Whatever you do, *never remain still.* You want to make sure you're constantly moving. Suppose it turns out part of your action plan requires that you sit still. In that case, you should compensate for this by going hard on the palpation, hand rubbing, and peering, and also amp up your vibration. Also, don't look into the distance for too long, as this can cause dissipation. Finally, if you find you've lost your place in the astral realm, don't sweat it. You can always re-enter the astral right away, no matter how often you lose it.

Astral Physics: Navigating the Space

You'll quickly find yourself falling in love with the physics of the astral plane because you don't have to deal with any of Earth's usual constraints, like gravity. Even when you encounter laws that seem to keep you in check, you can bend some of them with some effort. Still, there is some benefit to having a bit of physicality with you as you travel. For instance, it would be best to travel in a tangible form, much like your physical body. If you travel around without a form for too long, you will experience dissipation. Now, let's talk about what actions you can take in the astral.

- **You can move through solid objects.** Whatever it is, you want to fly, walk, swim, teleport, or move through it however you want. You can even move through other creatures as well. To do so successfully, you should be confident, like you've done this a million times before, and it will happen. If you're doubtful, you either won't get through, or you'll be stuck. If you get stuck, just squeeze your way out, or calm down and assume that attitude of having done this too many times already. You don't think too hard about sitting in a chair. You shouldn't overthink moving through solid objects, either.

- **You can fly.** There's nothing as thrilling as flying, defying gravity. This is one of the first things astral projectors learn and come to enjoy. However, you will need to master this. In the beginning, you may find it hard to get off the ground, and when you do, you might feel more like you're swimming through a viscous liquid rather than flying. Or you might find your problem isn't lift off, but control. You can fix this by becoming confident in your flying ability. Using your willpower, project yourself into the sky with a swift, powerful motion. Straining the body or brain is a great way to control your flight if you find you're moving too fast.

- **You can hover or float.** You're not flying in this case, just staying off the ground. To do this, just intend and imagine that you're floating off the ground, and you will immediately do so.

- **You can change your body.** Have fun adjusting your physical features. You can make yourself taller or shorter, take on a different gender, become an animal, change your hair or skin color, and so on. Begin with more minor changes, and then work your way up from there. If you have any issues at all, they're likely based on limited imagination and a lack of confidence. So be bold with this and look up images you'd like to become before you project.

- **You can modify some elements of your environment.** For instance, you could make a light bulb come on, or turn off, or change colors. Recall that you're in the astral plane and that some dimensions of this plane won't readily lend themselves to any changes you seek to create. With practice, you'll know what you can and can't change.

- **You can ditch the body.** No, not in a police procedural drama way. I mean, you don't have to travel around in a body. Remember, what you really are is consciousness, so you don't need a body to exist. However, the longer you're out of the body, the more likely you'll experience dissipation. To lose the body, you simply need to will it away. You'll notice the only senses you will use are sight and sound, and this is a blissful experience to have. You will also see you have 360-degree vision.

- **You can journey across universes in a matter of seconds.** You can think of a place, will yourself to be there, and there you are. You can point at a location, imagine the distance between it and your hand shrinking, and there you are. You can crouch down low, generate energy like a rocket, and then blast off to your chosen location in outer space in a single leap.

- **You can zoom in and out to explore worlds on your chosen scale.** You could shrink yourself till you're just a cell and interact with the world and entities on that scale. Just look at something for reference, like a grain of sand, and then will yourself zoom into it. You will find the sand grows bigger and bigger until you're at your desired level of shrinkage. You can also zoom out, using buildings or even whole planets as a reference point. So, the objects around you become smaller, and you can interact with beings on that magnitude of existence.

Translocation

When you quickly switch out one astral environment for another, this experience is called translocation. This tool is potent. You can use it to get where you need to quickly or take yourself out of undesirable situations or environments. It combines all the elements of solidification, prolonging the duration of your trip and maneuvering your astral environments. You can also use this to ramp up your awareness or lucidity to avoid dissipation, as you'll often wind up in a new environment that's even more stable than the former.

Usually, the process of translocation requires you to head back briefly to the midpoint between sleep and waking consciousness. This translates to temporarily blurry or lost vision, risking the chance that you will fully experience dissipation or experience a false awakening. It's a risk, but the more you practice, the better you'll get at it, and the less you have to worry.

You choose the environment you want to experience by using your willpower, intending yourself to be there. You can be as specific or as general as you want, in that you could choose to be on *any* mountain or on Mount Kinabalu itself. Note that the more general you are about where you want to be, the more variables you will run into in the new environment. You can also choose to keep your options open and simply will yourself to go somewhere new. Better yet, you can ask your guide to take you where they feel you should go at this stage in your life.

Translocation can move you to much more profound levels of awareness in the astral realm, as well as some exciting environments that can seem so vivid to the point that waking life looks like a cartoon. You'll also find that things are weirder, and your thought processes might be more bizarre too. The more you practice this in a session, the deeper the states you will uncover, to the point where you might forget to perform your solidification processes. With this in mind, make a point of constantly solidifying the new environment before you explore it.

The following are techniques you can use:

1. Dive headfirst, as mentioned before.

2. Spin on a head-to-toe axis.

3. Use portals. You can use any object as a portal or just use any door around you. You can will a door to appear wherever you want. You can also use a mirror, a window, or any liquid surface. With time, you can make a portal that looks just like in the movies, if you want. You can even use any cosmic object in the sky. Simply point at it and feel yourself zip-lining to it. As you approach it, it will probably look smaller than you expect, but it doesn't matter. Throw yourself into it forcefully, confidently expecting it to lead to where you want to go, and you'll be there.

Teleportation

This is translocation without any physical activity. Instead, you will yourself to a new place, using your imagination to help you. You might find this challenging; however, you simply need to close your eyes to make it work. This will help create the mini dissipation you need to successfully translocate, allowing you to refresh the scene to what you prefer. You may also do this with your eyes open, although you might find it difficult. For example, suppose you've seen special effects in a movie where a room morphs or melts into a different room. In that case, you can use this to your advantage and teleport with your eyes open, making sure to solidify as soon as you're in the new realm.

Fun Things to Do in the Astral Realm

1. Fly around your neighborhood.

2. Explore outer space.

3. Call on your guides and let them show you around.

4. Channel healing power to any body part.

5. Help heal a friend or relative from a distance by visiting them and flowing healing light to their body.

6. Meditate while in the astral realm for more powerful effects.

7. Conjure up scenarios you would like to happen in your life.

8. Request to be shown viable business ideas that would give you lots of money.

9. Visit loved ones who have passed on.

10. Intend to see your former lives or to check in on parallel ones.

11. Go to a school to rapidly accelerate your learning of any skill you're acquiring on Earth.

12. Intend to see a work of art or hear music that you can recreate on Earth.

13. Consort with the greats in your field, both living and dead, known and unknown.

14. Interact with other forms of life on micro and macro scales.

15. Rejuvenate your skin, so you look younger.

16. Get a sneak peek of possible future events that could play out in your life.

Chapter Sixteen: Problems and Mistakes to Overcome

Distracting Sounds

When projecting, you will hear voices or noises as you come out of your body. But no matter how loud they are, no matter what they're saying, ignore them. There's nothing to them.

Distracting Sensations

Even if you feel something touching you, hands grabbing you, someone holding you, ignore it all. None of this can hurt you, but it can break your focus and make you lose your nerve. If you let this stop you, you're not going to have any success with projections.

Fixing Poor Recall

Keep your first projections short and sweet. You only need ten to twenty seconds, and then you should get back in your body. That doesn't sound exciting, but it's necessary to improve your recall of future projections. What's the point in going on an hour-long adventure you'll soon forget? Train yourself by keeping the first few projections short and then writing down that brief experience.

The Pre-Projection Rush

Just when you're about to leave the physical, you might experience a surge of energy through your chest and stomach area, almost like you're very excited. This is the point where your astral body separates from the physical. You're almost there. Whatever you do, just remain calm, and don't react to the sensation when it hits you, or you'll wake up fully.

The Mind Split Effect

Remember, you are multidimensional. Suppose you notice that you've gone through all the vibrations, and all you feel is tired and groggy. In that case, your astral body exited, but you didn't notice because your consciousness was focused through your physical body, not both bodies. You might be paralyzed at this point. That's okay. Just stay calm, and wait for your astral body to return, remaining in that trance state. You must keep your mind clear as you wait for its return. When it returns, and your mind is free and clear, you will have full recollections of everything it was up to flooding your mind.

Mistakes to Avoid When Astral Projecting

Hopping from one method to another. Some people are impatient with the process and move from one system to another. You should stick with a technique for at least two to four weeks before deciding that it doesn't work for you. I understand you might be thinking, "Well, what if I stick with the wrong system for too long? Aren't I losing precious time?" To that, I say, the astral plane is going nowhere. To mitigate the risk of sticking with a method you don't resonate with, go through all the various ones and only choose whatever your gut tells you to try. It will always be there for you to explore. Also, spending time mastering a method is not a waste because you'll get better at learning to relax properly, which is absolutely essential for successful projection.

Trying to project at night. Not if you're new. This isn't the best time, as I've already mentioned before. Start with astral projecting when you wake up, then with time, you can project at night or whenever you feel like it.

Giving up because you've got no results yet. Some folks try once, and then they go, "That's it, doesn't work, I'm done." For example, I read a blog the other day by a lady who went for an astral projection class of sorts. The instructor basically had the students do visualization techniques, leading them to believe they had astral projected! If only the students had known, they were dealing with a real-life Barney, and all they did was use their imagination, not leave their bodies. Sadly, the lady wrote it off as something she'd never try again.

You may have read articles and research that disparage this phenomenon, but the only way to know is to prove it to yourself. If you've fallen victim to scammers, don't be quick to write this off. Instead, use what you now know and give it a go. Also, don't quit just because it didn't work the first few tries. Patience is your friend. Use affirmations to help you become more dedicated and consistent with your practice.

Confusing relaxation for the "body asleep" stage. Some beginners get into the deep relaxation stage and assume that means their body is asleep. That's not the same thing. You will know when your body is genuinely sleeping because you will experience hypnagogia, or hallucinatory sounds, images, and sensations. You will also notice you have no thoughts, and your sense of time is that it's slower, almost at a standstill. You will begin to feel the vibrations as well. So, don't attempt to leave your body in the relaxation stage.

Trying to project with a mind full of fear. Yes, you're doing something brand new, but you shouldn't let that frighten you. You can't get rid of the feeling of fear, but you *can* transmute it into excitement. Both emotions show up in your body the same way. The difference is in how you've chosen to look at this novel thing. Switch up your thoughts. For example, rather than think, "What if I don't come back into my body?" you could say, "If I don't come back on time, that means more time to explore!" Your attitude is critical. Also, it helps you to learn more about astral projection. The more you know, the less you have to be afraid of.

Indulging too much mind chatter. Don't ask yourself, "Am I doing this right? Is it okay for me to leave?" while you're trying to project. Instead, stop the inner chatter and just do it. An excellent way to stop your internal monologue is to listen. You can let thoughts fly by, remaining emotionally unattached to them. You can listen to the tiny ringing sound between your ears. You can turn your attention to your third eye. Whatever you do, don't attempt to silence your mind by force because that will just cause more thoughts to flow and disrupt your process. Instead, allow them to come and go with no judgment, and gently return your awareness to the task at hand.

Scratching itches and rolling over. We've covered this one before, but it is worth repeating. Leave that itch. It isn't a mosquito biting you, I promise. Also, don't roll over. If you do, recall that you already made sure your body was in a comfy, safe position before the process.

Being startled awake by loud knocking or sounds. This is a weird one that happens. I will admit that even I have fallen for it a few times myself, especially when I project in the day and am not home alone. Sometimes, you'll hear a loud knock or sound at the door, with someone you know or love calling you. If you've gotten to the point where you can now project at night, and it's about 11 pm or even 3 am, pause and ask yourself if there's anyone you know who'd come knocking at your door at that time. You'll learn not to fall for that trick and to continue with your projection.

Being too desperate. You want this magical experience. That's understandable, but you don't want to be so desperate for it that you suffer from performance anxiety every time you want to leave your body. So, relax, and be yourself, and you'll do just fine. You can affirm gently and lovingly, "I'm making this easy and having fun with it."

Improvising with your chosen method. You shouldn't change anything about the astral projection method you're using, at least not when you're just starting out. You can experiment later on when you've got the hang of it.

Trying to make this more complicated than it is. You may read other material about fancier ways to leave your body. Still, sometimes, the simple stuff works best, which is no exception for astral projection.

Giving up at incomplete separation. Just because your body is stuck doesn't mean you've failed. Instead, get more aggressive with your effort, and assure yourself with a calm confidence that this is easy for you.

Not realizing you're in the astral. This happens when you're in the real-time zone or when you don't get the sensation of separation from your body. This is why you should do reality checks to reduce the odds of this happening.

Not having strong intentions. If you want to succeed, then you will need willpower. When you wake up from sleep, your desire to project should be powerful, and you must keep all your conscious awareness on making that happen for you to get results. It can be a bit difficult because the tug of sleep or the day's schedule can be pretty intense, but you need to will yourself to see it through. Paradoxically, you need to be able to release this focus every now and then so that you can allow your body to slip back into sleep and then exit from there. Use the affirmation, "No matter what, I am astral projecting." Repeat this to yourself before bed and when you wake up as well.

Too many consecutive attempts. Go easy with this. Practice three days a week, or four at the most. Give yourself time in between your attempts so you don't feel too much pressure, which can make it hard for you to get to the restful stage. On days when you're not projecting, keep meditating. This will increase your level of awareness and make you more sensitive to subtler energies, a skill you need to master astral projection.

Troubleshooting Projection Problems

One of my astral hands is weaker than the other, so I can't use the rope technique. Your tactile awareness needs to be improved. Find somewhere you won't be disturbed for five minutes, and then lightly brush the back of each hand with the other, then stop. Next, sit with the feeling of your hands brushing each other. Attempt to generate that feeling without the physical brushing motion. Do this for at least five minutes a day, and you'll see improvements. You could also switch to a different technique in the meantime.

I keep getting distracted by the surge of energy in my torso. This happens just as your projection reflex kicks into gear, and you'll also feel vertigo along with the energy surge in your belly and chest. This surge of energy is from your lower chakras, and they help power your astral body so you can project. Just stay calm, and don't react to it. It won't hurt you. The more you project, the less intense the surge will be. You can also go on roller coaster rides or other adventures to help you get over the sensation.

When I'm in a trance, I feel cobwebs, stinging, and itching on my face and neck. As energy moves through the major and minor chakras all over your body, you might feel them as cobwebs or itching. Typically, the sensations match various acupuncture points in the face. The feeling will reduce bit by bit as you continue to work on projecting because you'll grow better at handling the increased energy flow. To help you with this, gently brush your face and then attempt to recreate the brushing sensation without touching your face. Amplify that feeling as much as you can, and if you lose it, brush your face again. Practice this for five to ten minutes daily and do the same exercise on your neck. Also, spray your room with bug spray before your projection sessions. This way, when you get those stinging, itching sensations, you know it's definitely not a mosquito or some other bug.

I feel pressure in my head. That's actually a good thing. It means your chakras are responding to the flow of energy that happens when you're going to project. So, ignore the pressure as best as you can.

It feels like there's a very tight band wrapped around my head. That's a sign of activity in your crown chakra. If you find that this is causing you migraines and headaches, then stop. Take a break. Try again in a few days. During your break, stimulate your crown and third eye chakras gently. Sit for just five minutes and feel for each one. The crown chakra is on top of your head, while the third eye is between your eyes, slightly above both brows.

I get the feeling of choking or being strangled. If you feel pressure on your chest and throat, it's usually because your heart and throat chakras are at work. If you don't have enough oxygen, this could be due to sleep apnea, where you stop breathing in your sleep and then suddenly gasp for air when your oxygen levels are too low. Trance will help you notice whatever issues you have with breathing in sleep. You could try to position your head so that it's tilted back. This way, your airways are more open. That said, do speak with your doctor about this.

I keep getting stuck to my body at my legs/head/stomach. Avoid eating heavy protein meals before you project. Digestion takes a lot of energy, so the heavier the meal, the more the energy is funneled to the digestive process. Your astral body shuts down for an hour or longer when you've had an enormous feast, and your chakras can slow down to the point of inactivity. So cut down on huge meals, especially heavy protein, when you want to leave your body. Also, take off any jewelry you have on. Your astral body has no issues passing through objects, but for some reason, having jewelry on can interfere with your astral body's exit.

No matter what I do, I can't see properly once I'm out of my body. One of the leading causes of poor astral vision is a lack of energy flow into the astral body. The best way to deal with this problem is to draw energy from your physical body. It's a simple thing to do and has proven to be adequate time and time again. Just feel yourself drawing power from your physical body, and that energy will flow. You can visualize or imagine golden or bluish-white light flowing from your body through your silver cord to your astral double. If you can't find your silver cord, just imagine being energized by light.

- Conjure a lamp or torch in your hand.
- Move to a different room with more lighting.
- Say, "Light now!" or "Clarity now!" With a confident attitude.
- Leave a lamp on before you project.
- Imagine light suddenly flooding the room.
- Teleport to a location you know is well-lit.
- Only project during the day.

I keep encountering scary creatures or beings. First things first, stop being afraid when you project. No one can hurt you. Second, you need to be brave. The next time a creature or being makes you uncomfortable, you can imagine a blindingly bright light radiating from your heart chakra, blasting all around you. Feel it envelop you like the most comfortable blanket ever.

Another thing you can do is look at that being and feel intense love for yourself and for them too. They won't be able to stand it, and they'll leave you alone. If they are only your thought forms, they will fade into nothing. So, if you're feeling courageous, give them a big hug and really amp up the love in your heart.

Chapter Seventeen: Exiting Strategies

A question that gets asked a lot is how do you come back from the astral plane? It's an understandable concern, which only exists because there have been many misrepresentations of astral projection in the media and myths perpetuated by the ignorant.

There's no reason to worry about your soul getting stuck somewhere or not knowing how to get back to your body. You will never return to find someone or something else has taken up residence in your body because these things do not happen. In fact, it's even harder to leave your body than it is for you to get back to it. So, to understand why you have nothing to fear, let's talk about the silver cord in detail.

After my first few conscious projections many years ago, I realized that the trouble with leaving my body wasn't staying out as long as I could. For a very long time, I struggled with trying to prolong the experience. I wasn't in the best place in my life back then, so you can understand why I'd want to just escape to the astral plane and remain there forever if I could.

What I soon learned was that this wasn't a unique struggle. It's something a lot of astral travelers have to deal with. That's why you'll find no end of material talking about how to deepen your experience or extend your stay in the astral realm. If you don't get back because of dissipation, it'll be someone knocking on your door or Mother Nature's call to take a whiz. So, you need not fear being stuck in the astral plane. One way or another, you'll return to the physical.

As I've mentioned before, if you get too excited or scared, you will find yourself back in your physical body. If you can't exit, you can just generate an intense feeling of excitement. Of course, you don't need a reason to feel excited, but if it helps you, you can think of one, so you're immediately booted back to the ordinary world. Want to stay longer? Then keep your mood even and calm, in addition to doing the solidifying exercises.

The Silver Cord

This is a literal cord that connects your body and soul together. It's this same cord that shows you the way back to your body when in the astral plane. You may or may not see it, but it's there. No one can cut it, no matter how "powerful" they are. It's no ordinary cord. It gives your body life from your higher self, allowing its consciousness to flow into your physical body, as well as your other bodies.

The cord is connected to your body at different points, depending on your present projection. Usually, they are connected to major chakra points. However, Robert Bruce describes them as connected to a convergence of strands that all lead out of the major chakras and a few minor ones.

The silver cord is eternal. The only time it gets severed is if you die—and you're not going to die from any experience in the astral plane, just to put the kibosh on that lie right away. Furthermore, it stretches endlessly, so even if you somehow journey light-years away from your body, it won't matter. It has no limits.

No one can destroy your cord—not even you. When you project, you could try and see for yourself. You can't break it or tear it, and while you'd assume all that traveling should tangle it, it doesn't wind up in knots. It is made of pure energy, which cannot be destroyed. This cord also makes sure that your body is yours and yours alone, so you don't have to worry about someone else possessing it.

Coming Back from the Astral Realm

To return, all you have to do is follow your silver cord. That's it. If you can't find it, don't panic. The mere thought of your body will return you to it. Just intend with willpower that you'd like to return to your body, and you'll be there. Remember, we've talked about the physics of this realm. Concepts like space and time don't work the same way they do on Earth, so you don't have to worry about taking forever to find your body or teleport to it. You can trace your route back with the cord without worrying years have gone by, and your loved ones think you're in a coma at best or dead, at worst. You can speed up the process. It's all up to you.

Another worry you might have is finding your way back home, especially if the cord isn't visible to you. But, again, this realm is responsive to thought. So, it's none of your business where you are relative to your bedroom. You can be back home in the blink of an eye.

Keeping a positive state of mind before you leave your body will ensure you don't have any issues with getting back when you need to. If you leave your body while feeling like crap, that's okay. Just remember that regardless of what's happening around you at any moment in time, you can choose to radiate light and love in thought and energy. Doing that will fix things right up and help you get back home. If you'd rather be able to see your silver cord all the time, then you only need to imagine it's there, and it will show up for you.

Other Ways to Exit the Astral Realm

Have an intense emotional reaction. You can drum up the memory of something that makes you very emotional. If you're very in tune with your feelings, you can just generate the emotion without context. And that will cause you to return to your body.

Make your body tense. How is this different from straining your body? To be clear, when I say "strain your body" to solidify your environment, I mean your *astral* body. When it comes to your exit, you should strain your *physical* one. You have a connection to it, even from the astral. So the intention to strain your muscles will be communicated to the physical body through the silver cord.

High Awareness Level: Critical for Exit

When your level of awareness is too low, sometimes you can be in a projection and then slip into a state of partial lucidity. In this state, you forget you're projecting and that you're in charge, and you can get swept up in what's happening around you. This is what causes you to have very intense "dreams" (I quote the word dreams because you think you're dreaming, but you aren't) where you feel trapped and seemingly can't wake up no matter what you do.

Downloading Your Memories to Your Brain

As you prepare to exit the astral realm, you should mentally note a few keywords that summarize your experience, just like you do with a dream journal. Or, better yet, you can write out the keywords as you begin the exit process so that you can remember them when you awaken.

Suppose your physical body is awake even a little when the astral one re-enters it. In that case, you will feel energy rushing through you, bringing the physical to full awareness. It's rapid and feels almost like an adrenaline rush moving up from your lower body to your stomach and chest and then coming to an abrupt halt.

When you get these sensations, this is the best time to download the memories of your astral trip to your physical brain, so you don't forget it. What you must do is generate an intense feeling of needing to remember something, and then the keywords you shouted should come back to you.

Sit up and put your feet on the ground, and then use every effort you can to recall all keywords and all the memories. Don't give up. They're there, and you just need to pull them out. Usually, when you find even a piece, the rest of the experiences you had in the astral realm will come flooding back to you. You may find it helpful to work your way backward, meaning remember the last thing that happened, and then the thing before that, till you get to the memory of leaving your body.

The best way to make sure you always remember your trips is to time them yourself and exit deliberately rather than wait for dissipation. So, in the astral realm, solidify your world as you execute your plan. Then, when you're done, exit that world on your own terms. Don't take longer than you need. This will ensure you remember every last detail of your trip.

Remember the mind split? It comes into play here. As you return to your body, keep your awareness clear in the astral form. Do your best to ignore the intense sensations you have as you re-enter because those can cause you to break your concentration and forget your keywords. Your intention to hold your awareness in your astral form must be firm as you re-enter. Don't allow that body to succumb to the surges of energy it will feel as it gets back into your physical one. It must maintain its focus on where it's been, what it's been up to. You can shout out a trigger phrase to help you as you re-enter, like, "The Buddha laughs," if you happened to have a conversation with the Buddha on laughter or something.

Falling during Sleep

Have you ever been in bed, falling asleep, when you suddenly jerked on the bed because you felt like you were literally falling, so you wake up and "catch" yourself? This can happen a few times before you finally do sleep off. The cause of this sensation is a brief exit and re-entry of the astral body.

Suppose you notice you're very lethargic and heavy after this falling sensation. In that case, your astral body has likely left the building, so to speak. On the other hand, if you wake up fully and catch yourself, then it's back in. If the former is the case, hold a firm intention in your mind that you will immediately return to your body when you find yourself in the astral realm. Tell yourself you will yell out a trigger phrase while doing so. This will help you learn what your astral body has been up to and help you get better at downloading your memories.

Do you constantly get that falling sensation? Then next time, try to stay up a little longer than you normally would, keeping your consciousness between sleep and wakefulness. For example, you can hold up your forearms with the elbows on the bed so that when you fall asleep, your hands will slip and wake you up. This way, you have a better chance of recalling any astral experience you may have.

The One Time You Can't Return

If you attempt to re-enter your body and find you can't, chances are your physical body has entered into a deep sleep. In this stage of sleep, your astral body is temporarily locked out, and you might get the sense that your body died while you were away. If you reached out to touch your physical body, it would feel cold, almost like a corpse.

Any physical noise will cause your physical body to wake up, and then that will allow your astral body to get back in. When this happens, you get a sense of intense terror and dread when you wake up, and the memories flood your mind instantly, so you recall everything. You might find yourself dreading astral projection after this experience.

Now you know what's going on when you can't get in. You shouldn't allow yourself to feel fear. Understand this happens very often with projectors all over the world and that you're in no danger. So why not take advantage of the extra time you have? Go on even more journeys and tick off whatever other plans you might have had for the next projection.

Don't conclude that you're dead just because you can't re-enter your body. If you don't see any late relatives and friends, or religious figures, angels, or other friends from past lives, then you're probably just in a deep sleep. Don't panic.

Robert Bruce's Flicker Tape Method

This is a great one to use, especially when you want to make sure you recall everything you experienced. It's also helpful when your early tries at leaving your body don't work out or when you miss an astral exit and have no idea whether or not you were successful. You can use this method to wake up, and it's better than using a regular alarm.

Record a tapping sound using your phone or computer. For example, you want to tap your wooden desk very lightly. Use just one tap per second for five seconds. Allow ten seconds of silence and record slightly louder taps once each second for just five seconds. Allow another ten seconds to go by. The next series of taps need to be a chinking sound, light as possible. You can tap a pen against a coffee mug, or glass, for five seconds, tapping once each second. Then allow another ten seconds to pass by.

The next series of tapes should be slightly louder, still in the same format as before. You may move on to progressively sharper sounds, going as far as banging a spoon against a metal pot. You could use a xylophone or any sounds you like to keep things interesting. When you're done recording, you can set this up at your preferred volume as an alarm.

When you're out of your body, you should remain about six meters or twenty feet away from it, so you're not sucked back in. If you notice there's some pressure trying to reel you back in, resist it, and move as quickly as you can away from your body. Better yet, if there's another clock in the house, you can go to that other room and monitor it, waiting to enter your body. Then, when the alarm goes off, return to the room to re-enter your body.

Keep in mind that your physical body can be anywhere from light, medium to deep sleep. Keep your re-entry phrase firmly in your mind as you wait for the tugging sensations, which means your body is starting to wake up. As soon as you feel the tug, slide into your physical body as you yell out your phrase with intense emotion. Your intention should be to take charge of your physical body and force it to wake up, so you can write down your experience. Needless to say, your journal should be well within reach.

It is my sincere hope that with this final chapter, I've been able to thoroughly allay any fears you've had that have made you shy away from leaving your body. The door is open now. You need only walk through it, and you already know how.

Bonus: Astral Travel Daily Practice Calendar

Here's a calendar of daily practices you can use to prime yourself for a successful exit from your body. You only need fifteen minutes per day: five minutes for the affirmations, five for the meditations, and five for your mindfulness exercises.

Then, **you're going to record your dreams every time you wake up for the next 30 days.** Again, if all you remember is one image, write it down. If you don't remember dreaming, just write down how you feel, and trust that you will begin to recall your dreams in full.

Day 1

Affirmation: I am aware I exist in multiple dimensions of existence.

Meditation: sit with your eyes shut and observe your breath.

Mindfulness exercise: sit with your eyes open, and just notice your body. Look at your hands and the rest of your visible body with a detached state, like it's a vehicle. Then, ponder this question: "Who is looking through my eyes?"

Day 2

Affirmation: I am always aware of my body as it goes to sleep.

Meditation: close your eyes, lie down, and observe your breath.

Mindfulness exercise: walk from one spot to another. Shut your eyes. In your mind, recreate the sensation of walking from where you were to where you are, feeling your feet against the floor, your body pushing against the air. Open your eyes and walk back to the first spot. Close your eyes and recreate the movement again. Make sure you account for the change in location in your imagination.

Day 3

Affirmation: I am conscious as I separate from my body while it sleeps.

Meditation: sit and look at the back of your hands. Brush each one with the other. For five minutes, continue to brush your hands, but in your mind. You should feel your awareness in your hands increasing.

Mindfulness exercise: pay attention to your thoughts. Ask yourself each time you make an assumption, "But is it true? Do I want that to be true? Do I accept that as my truth?"

Day 4

Affirmation: I am far more than just my physical body.

Meditation: sit and close your eyes. Imagine a surge of white energy flooding your physical body in a straight line from your root chakra. See it moving on up through the midpoint of your belly, chest, throat, and third eye chakras, and then out the top of your head.

Mindfulness exercise: say your name out loud. Listen to your voice and notice how it sounds. Then, repeat your name again, this time as though you were addressing someone else, not yourself.

Day 5

Affirmation: I recall everything I do in the astral plane when I wake up.

Meditation: sit and close your eyes. Focus on your breath. Halfway through the time, feel yourself sitting in a different chair, facing a different wall. You should feel it in your body and mind that you're in this other position.

Mindfulness exercise: at the end of your day, recall everything that happened during your day by working your way backward, from when you hit the bed to when you brushed your teeth for bed, and on and on. Continue till the moment you woke up in the morning.

Day 6

Affirmation: I always receive value from every projection I have.

Meditation: shut your eyes and listen to the sounds around you, with no judgment and no attempt to figure out what it all means.

Mindfulness exercise: lie down. Close your eyes. From a first-person perspective, see yourself outside your home. Walk into your house, and head right to where you're lying down. Look at yourself as though you're a stranger. Notice the rising and falling of your chest as you breathe.

Day 7

Affirmation: I remain in complete control of all my astral experiences.

Meditation: sit with your eyes shut, and keep your awareness centered on your heart chakra, right in the middle of your chest.

Mindfulness exercise: close your eyes. Generate a falling sensation within yourself. Think about what it's like to go down a roller coaster or in an elevator and create that sensation—alternate between intensifying the falling feeling and slowing it down.

Day 8

Affirmation: I own my mind. I use my mind to do my will.

Meditation: sit in silence for five minutes, and contemplate the vastness of the universe, and sit with the fact that the universe is within you, not outside you.

Mindfulness exercise: every time you notice something negative cross your mind today, your job is to observe your emotions detachedly. Acknowledge they are there, and just watch them. Don't act on them. Instead, choose to do something that's the complete opposite of your usual reaction.

Day 9

Affirmation: whatever I will into being is done.

Meditation: sit in silence. Shut your eyes and allow yourself to be overwhelmed with a feeling of gratitude and completeness for no reason.

Mindfulness exercise: pay attention to your thoughts. Ask yourself each time you make an assumption, "But is it true? Do I want that to be true? Do I accept that as my truth?"

Day 10

Affirmation: I am light as a feather, steady as a rock.

Meditation: sit for five minutes, observing your breath.

Mindfulness exercise: play with feeling heavy, then feeling light. Alternate the two of them. Allow any imagery that corresponds with these sensations to come up in your mind. Notice how your body translates those sensations.

Day 11

Affirmation: the only "where" is here.

Meditation: Stand outside with bare feet. If you can stand on bare earth, even better. Shut your eyes and just breathe. Ground yourself in the moment.

Mindfulness exercise: pick a spot to sit and watch people from. In your imagination, reach out and touch the hands of people across the street from you. You can also touch objects. Practice holding them with your mind's hands. Feel their textures and shapes. Notice their heft.

Day 12

Affirmation: the only "when" is now.

Meditation: for this meditation, don't time yourself. Just sit still until you start to notice that you can't really sense how fast or slow time is, if it even exists at all. When you get this sensation, take a few deep breaths, and then come out of meditation.

Mindfulness exercise: go the whole day without looking at your watch. If you're at work and your job is time-sensitive, pick a time when you know you won't be bothered to do this. Every time you get the itch to look at what the clock says, affirm, "The only 'when' is now."

Day 13

Affirmation: nothing means anything, except what I believe it means.

Meditation: sit in silence, listening to the sounds around you. When your mind tries to ascribe it a meaning, origin, or label, let it go.

Mindfulness exercise: your exercise is to imagine a different meaning for what you hear, whether it's a song on the radio, a friend talking to you, or the news. Deliberately apply a meaning you prefer or even one you don't. Observe what happens within your mind.

Day 14

Affirmation: I am deliberate about the meanings I assign to things.

Meditation: sit with your eyes open. Look around the room at various objects and let go of all the descriptions and meanings your mind tries to assign them.

Mindfulness exercise: pick one color. Every time you see it today, in your mind's eye, give it a different color.

Day 15

Affirmation: I am in tune with my astral body.

Meditation: sit with your eyes shut and notice all the sensations you feel, within and without. When your mind tries to label it, whether it's an itch, a twinge, or subtle energy, don't dwell on your mind's definitions. Let it go.

Mindfulness exercise: for five minutes, have a friend tickle you with something light and feathery. You'll want to laugh, but ask yourself, "Do I have to?" Just sit and observe the sensation. You must do nothing. Don't try to stop them.

Start again from day 1 for the next couple of weeks.

Day 31 is when you should make your first attempt at astral projection. Do the exercises that resonate with you, and then take time to read through your dream journal. Allow yourself to sink into the memories, to immerse yourself in it as you would a novel or a movie. Then, using your preferred method of projection, leave your body.

If you're successful, make sure you only stay out for just ten to twenty seconds, solidifying the state, and then deliberately re-enter your body. That should be your only plan on the first try.

On subsequent tries, make a plan about what you want to do, have a backup plan if you can't execute for some reason, or have more time in the astral realm because your body is in a deep sleep. If you're unsure what to do with yourself, refer to chapter fifteen for ideas on what you can do in the astral plane.

If you're not successful, don't panic. Instead, do one more week of your daily astral practice, and then try again.

Conclusion

This book ends here, but it's the start of the rest of your life, for sure. Before we wrap up, I want to stress that you shouldn't quit just because you didn't leave your body the first few times. Some people get it right away, but others need more time. It's the same with any skill. Please be patient with the process and be patient with yourself too. Suppose you beat yourself up about not getting it right. In that case, you're only prolonging the process, setting yourself up for disappointment at best or permanent skepticism at worst. That would be like seeing the gates to the city of gold, locking them up with your own hands, and throwing the keys away.

Now, I know you probably looked at that bonus section and decided you're not going to wait a whole month to leave your body. I get why you'd feel that way. You want to keep the momentum going, knowing what you now know, and that is commendable! Here's the thing, though: you have to give this time. Lay the groundwork first, and that will improve the odds of your success wildly. The exercises you've been given are insanely powerful. They will give back to you in ways you couldn't possibly imagine if you invest the time and do them first.

Don't feel tempted to freestyle the exit or entry methods when you're first starting out. You have all the time in the world to follow your own hunches and experiment, but for now, you should get used to the projection process first. It's like you've never driven a car in your life, and you suddenly decide to hop into a car and make like you're starring in a *Fast and Furious* movie. Naturally, you won't like how it ends. In the same way, please follow all instructions to the letter so you don't run into any problems you could have avoided.

On that note, please keep your first few projections to no more than twenty seconds. The most successful projectors have followed this rule to the letter. You must take charge of your re-entry; otherwise, you'll just have a bunch of fantastic experiences that you don't even remember.

Respect other people's privacy and respect the beings you meet. If you run into anyone who feels off, remember to affirm that you're light and love and get on with your business. Don't be hostile or fearful, no matter what. Remember, nothing and no one can harm you in the astral plane.

Every consistent projector will tell you with no hesitation that the quality of their life has improved immensely since learning this skill. In love, family, career, health, and every other way, the effects of astral projection are very noticeable. Astral projection will help you live life with the full awareness that you are more than physical. You will know that death is simply a portal to more adventures and that you are an infinite being. This first-hand knowledge helps you lighten up and enjoy your present existence. What could be better than that?

The critical difference between astral projection and death is that you have a body to go back to in the former case. Astral projection will teach you that there is nothing to fear and will show you just how truly free you are. Imagine a world where everyone ditched the ideas they got from *Insidious* (2010) or *Behind Her Eyes* (2021) and learned to explore the truth for themselves. Imagine a world no longer crippled by the fear of death, where everyone is well aware of their limitless nature. This is why I've done my little bit in writing this book, in the hopes that we all one day will wake up to the truth of who we really are.

You see, most projectors radiate a sense of peace that just goes beyond understanding, even in the "toughest" situations in life. They have the most creative solutions to problems, and they know how to use their astral selves to manifest their desires in the physical realm because they understand the concept, "As above, so below." So, if you want something to happen in the physical world, create that scenario in the astral realm. Then, trust that your action on that plane will influence your "real" life; this is more than enough to create whatever changes you seek.

You can heal troublesome ailments and pains in your body and help others to heal as well. You can play out a problem in the astral plane and intend for the solution to make itself visible to you. You can confer with a guide, a deceased relative, or a friend if you prefer, and ask for their counsel. If you've lost something, you can find it. If you need business ideas that will yield good money, you can get them there. If you want to understand your past lives better or peek in on your alternate selves to see if there's something they're doing that you could learn from or emulate, you can too. This is the realm of infinite possibilities.

Finally, you have all of this information now, but it does absolutely no good if you just keep it in your head without putting it to work. You have to be consistent with this to see results. You must be disciplined about your daily routine. There's no other way around this. Don't be put off, though, because you're going to find the rewards are well worth it in the end. So be bold. Dare to explore this new frontier of life, and you'll find yourself richly rewarded.

Here's another book by Silvia Hill that you might like

Free Bonus from Silvia Hill available for limited time

Hi Spirituality Lovers!

My name is Silvia Hill, and first off, I want to THANK YOU for reading my book.

Now you have a chance to join my exclusive spirituality email list so you can get the ebooks below for free as well as the potential to get more spirituality ebooks for free! Simply click the link below to join.

P.S. Remember that it's 100% free to join the list.

~~$27~~ FREE BONUSES

- 9 Types of Spirit Guides and How to Connect to Them
- How to Develop Your Intuition: 7 Secrets for Psychic Development and Tarot Reading
- Tarot Reading Secrets for Love, Career, and General Messages

Access your free bonuses here

https://livetolearn.lpages.co/sh-astral-projection-for-beginners-paperback/

References

Bruce, Robert. *Astral Dynamics: A NEW Approach to Out-of-Body Experience.* Charlotte, VA: Hampton Roads, 1999.

Crow, John L. "Taming the astral body: The Theosophical Society's ongoing problem of emotion and control", *Journal of the American Academy of Religion.* 2012.

Kemp, Harold. *Past Lives, Dreams, and Soul Travel.* Eckankar. Minneapolis, MN. 2003.

LA Berge, Stephen. *Lucid Dreaming.* New York: Ballantine, 1985.

Mercury, Daniel. *Becoming Half Hidden: Shamanism and Initiation among the Inuit.* Act Universities Stockholmiensis. Stockholm Studies in Comparative Religion. Stockholm: Almqvist & Wiksell. 1985.

Novak, Peter. *The Lost Secret of Death: Our Divided Souls and the Afterlife.* Charlotte, VA: Hampton Roads, 2003.

Bruce, Robert. *Practical Psychic Self-Defense: Understanding and Surviving Unseen Influences.* Charlotte, VA: Hampton Roads, 2002.

Rawcliffe, Donovan. *Occult and Supernatural Phenomena.* Dover Publications, 1988.

Bruce, Robert. *Astral Dynamics: A New Approach to Out-of-Body Experiences.* Hampton Roads Publishing.

Monroe, Robert. *Journeys Out of the Body Doubleday.* Reprinted (1989) Souvenir Press Ltd. 1971.

Muldoon, Sylvan and Carrington, Hereward. *Projection of the Astral Body*. Rider and Company. 1929.

Hines, Terence. *Pseudoscience and the Paranormal*. Prometheus Books. 2003.

Gilovich, Thomas. *How We Know What Isn't So: The Fallibility of Human Reason in Everyday Life*. 1993

Time-Life Books (ed). *Psychic Voyages. Mysteries of the Unknown*. Alexandria, VA: Time-Life Books, 1987.

Made in the USA
Las Vegas, NV
14 January 2025

16373183R00105